I'm delighted to have the opportunity to talk to yo mastering prompts when using artificial intelligence to achiev with, let me point out that tools like ChatGPT, LLAMA advanced machine learning models developed by privat META, ANTHROPIC or GOOGLE. They are designed to gener... to have been written by a human, based on the prompt or prompt you give it. This is an impressive achievement and breakthrough in the field of artificial intelligence, and it opens the door to a plethora of already well-exploited applications, but above all to almost limitless potential.

A key aspect of using ChatGPT or other similar models effectively is understanding how to formulate your prompts to get the type of response you're looking for. A well-formulated prompt can help guide this intelligent program in a specific direction, giving it valuable information about the context and content you're looking for.

The aim of this book is to give you all the information you need to master the conversational aspect of AI, and to better understand the inner workings of this fast-growing field. The ability to formulate prompts well can also help you avoid some of the limitations of artificial intelligence. By carefully formulating your prompts, you can help guide the AI to more precise and useful answers for you with the desired result.

The AI will then provide you with the right answer if you have formulated it well, and this will be increasingly true in the future with the exponential development of these capabilities. It's becoming clear that mastering prompts when using an AI can not only help you achieve more accurate and relevant results, but also fully exploit the creative and informative capabilities of this artificial intelligence tool, as you'll quickly see incredible renderings can be achieved.

Whether you're an entrepreneur looking for new product ideas, a writer looking for inspiration for a story, or simply someone looking to find out more about a particular subject, mastering ChatGPT's prompts can be an invaluable asset in achieving results that were unimaginable just a few years ago.

The potential impact of artificial intelligence, according to Bill Gates, is such that this visionary technologist envisages a profound transformation of our society under its influence. Gates anticipates a technological revolution that will reshape the way we work, learn, travel, heal and communicate. Not only that, but he also predicts that entire industries will reorganize to adapt to this new reality, with the effective use of AI as a hallmark of success for companies.

But that's not all. Gates envisions a future where artificial intelligence not only optimizes our existing systems, but also acts as a powerful driver of social justice and equity. For Microsoft's founding father, intelligent programs have the potential to benefit almost every area of our society, including those fighting against some of the world's most glaring inequalities. He envisions, for example, artificial intelligence that could save millions of lives by preventing child deaths from preventable diseases like diarrhea and malaria. And it's not just global health that could benefit from AI. Gates firmly believes that this technology can play a major role in our fight against climate change. "I'm convinced that the intelligent machine can make the world a fairer place," he declared.

A conviction that reinforces the idea that this revolutionary technology has the potential to bring about not only technological change, but also profound societal transformations. Yes, the intelligent machine presents challenges and risks, but it also offers immense potential to transform our world in a positive way.

Imagine a world where every student has access to a personalized teacher, where every patient has the possibility of accurate diagnosis and appropriate treatment, where scientific advances are accelerated by AI that can process volumes of data beyond human capacity. The intelligent agent has the potential to help us solve some of the most complex and pressing problems facing our world, from climate change to poverty.

As we continue to move forward into this new era, it's important to remember that the conversational model is a tool, and it's up to us as human beings to decide how we use it. If we are wise, ethical and considerate of the well-being of all, AI can help us create a better future for humanity. So let's move forward with hope, determination and a deep respect for the value and dignity of every person. The future is in our hands, and with the help of artificial intelligence, we have the potential to achieve truly extraordinary things.

In this book, which I've taken pleasure in writing with the help of AIs, you'll find all the information you need to understand and use this revolutionary new technology to your advantage.

You'll discover step-by-step how it works, and how to make the most of the intelligent machine's capabilities by writing relevant prompts and discovering new abilities in a wide range of fields. Artificial intelligence is becoming more and more global. It's no longer the stuff of science fiction movies, it's now science, and the future is now.

Table of contents

Version 1.3 completed in July 2023

-1-

History and creation of AI models

"Artificial intelligence will help us solve our society's most challenging problems."

Yoshua Bengio

From the beginnings of AI to the dawn of language models

The beginnings of artificial intelligence:

Artificial intelligence as we know it today has its roots in the pioneering work of many scientists and researchers. Among them, Alan Turing, a British mathematician, is often cited as the father of theoretical computing and artificial intelligence. In the 1930s, Turing designed a theoretical machine, known today as the Turing machine, which is capable of solving any computable problem, provided it can be expressed as an algorithm. This theoretical conception is fundamental to the development of the modern computer.

The concept of the Turing Test is simple: a human interrogator communicates with a human and a machine without knowing which is which. If, after a series of questions, the interrogator cannot determine with certainty which is the machine, then the machine has passed the test. In other words, if a machine manages to convince a human that it is as human as its real-life opponent, it is considered to have demonstrated some form of intelligence. Despite its renown, the Turing Test has generated significant controversy. Its critics argue that it assesses a machine's ability to imitate human intelligence, rather than its true intelligence. For example, a machine could pass the Turing Test simply by being programmed with sufficiently convincing answers, without really understanding the questions or the underlying concepts. What's more, the Turing Test ignores certain forms of intelligence that are difficult to assess through dialogue, such as spatial or emotional intelligence. So a machine could fail the Turing Test, but excel in other forms of intelligence.

Although criticized, the Turing Test has had an undeniable impact on the development of AI. It provided artificial intelligence researchers with a concrete goal, and helped popularize the concept among the general public. In addition, the challenges raised by the Turing Test stimulated innovation in terms of intelligent machines, pushing researchers to develop systems capable of understanding and responding in a more human way. The idea of a machine capable of thinking like a human was popularized by the "Turing Test", introduced by Turing himself in his 1950 article, "Computing Machinery and Intelligence". In this test, if a machine manages to convince a human interrogator that it is also human, then it can be said to have demonstrated some form of intelligence. It's a concept that continues to influence the way we measure artificial intelligence to this day.

Neural networks and the perceptron

The adventure of artificial intelligence took an interesting turn with the introduction of the first neural networks and the perceptron. An artificial neural network is a computer model inspired by the functioning of neurons in the human brain. The perceptron, introduced by Frank Rosenblatt in 1957, is a type of artificial neural network and can be considered the ancestor of modern neural networks. It was the first model capable of learning from its mistakes, a revolutionary idea at the time.

The perceptron is a binary supervised learning algorithm. Designed to take several binary inputs, the perceptron weights and sums them, then passes the total through an activation function to produce an output. This output is also binary, which means that the perceptron is used for binary classification tasks, where the aim is to classify a data set into two distinct groups.

The perceptron algorithm is relatively simple and intuitive. It starts by assigning random weights to the inputs, then adjusts these weights according to the errors it makes in classifying the training data. If the perceptron's output is correct, the weights remain the same. If the output is incorrect, the weights are adjusted accordingly.

This weight adjustment process is repeated several times, until the perceptron succeeds in classifying the training data correctly, or until a maximum number of iterations is reached. The perceptron has some important limitations, for example it can only handle linearly separable problems. That is, if the two classes of data cannot be separated by a straight line (or, in higher-dimensional spaces, a hyperplane), the perceptron will not be able to find a solution.

This limitation has led to the development of more sophisticated models such as multi-layer neural networks, which can solve non-linear problems. The perceptron has had a profound impact on the development of AI and Machine Learning. As one of the first machine learning algorithms, it laid the foundations for today's more sophisticated models.

In addition, the perceptron served as a basic model for the construction of artificial neural networks, which are now at the heart of numerous applications, from image recognition to machine translation.

The winters and springs of AI

The history of artificial intelligence is rich and complex, punctuated by a series of exciting advances and disconcerting setbacks. These phases of optimism and disappointment, known as the "springs" and "winters" of AI, have shaped the landscape as we know it today.

Think of the evolution of the intelligent machine as a succession of seasons. AI "springs" are flourishing periods of technological progress, exciting discoveries and increased investment. By contrast, AI "winters" are chilly periods of growing skepticism, palpable dissatisfaction and declining funding.

The first "winter" of artificial intelligence took place in the 1970s, after an initial phase of enthusiasm. During this period, the dream of creating intelligent machines met with brutal reality. The challenges inherent in automatic language translation, natural language understanding and general problem solving proved far greater than anticipated. What began as a springtime of hope turned into a harsh winter of disillusionment.

This period is best remembered for the "Machine Translation" project launched in the 1960s. Researchers hoped that machines would soon be able to master translation between human languages. However, they soon realized that translation required a contextual and cultural understanding that was beyond the capacity of machines at the time. The project was eventually abandoned, contributing to the advent of the first AI winter.

The second "winter" of artificial intelligence followed in the 1980s and early 1990s. During this period, the enthusiasm for "expert systems" - programs designed to mimic human reasoning in specific fields - cooled. Despite their initial promise, these systems showed their limitations. They could not generalize their learning to new situations, which severely limited their usefulness. But every winter has always been followed by a new spring. The emergence of deep learning in the early 2000s revolutionized this field. This approach, based on artificial neural networks, has made it possible to achieve unprecedented levels of performance in tasks such as image and speech recognition.

A prominent example is DeepMind's AlphaGo, which in 2016 beat the world champion in the game of Go, a challenge long considered insurmountable for machines. This victory marked the beginning of a new springtime for the intelligent machine, a period of innovation and progress that continues to this day.

The history of artificial intelligence is a story of cycles, of ups and downs, of springs and winters. The early days of AI, from the Turing machine to neural networks and the perceptron, laid the foundations for the revolutions we are living through today. Each era, despite its challenges, has brought new innovations and discoveries, shaping the intelligent machine we know and use today. So, while history has shown that winter will eventually come, every winter is followed by a spring, heralding a new era of opportunity and discovery in the world of artificial intelligence.

The early days of AI, from the Turing machine to neural networks and the perceptron, laid the foundations for the revolutionary advances we see today. Despite the ups and downs, each era has brought its own innovations and discoveries, paving the way for the intelligent machine we know and use today.

The Evolution of AI: From symbolic approaches to deep learning

Over the last few decades, the field of artificial intelligence has undergone a rapid evolution, moving from symbolic methods to highly sophisticated deep learning techniques. Understanding this evolution is essential to grasping the transformative nature of modern AI.

Symbolic AI:

In the vast world of artificial intelligence, symbolic AI, often referred to as "good old-fashioned AI" (GOFAI), occupies a special place. This traditional approach, which marked the first steps of this technology, uses clear and explicit symbolic representations to solve problems and understand the world around us. The symbolic intelligent machine is built on a defined architecture of rules and symbols that embody real-world entities or concepts. These symbols, explicitly coded, are used to build models representing the world, like a child using blocks to build a representation of a house. The aim is to solve problems by manipulating these symbols, applying logical rules to move from an initial to a final state, or to solve a puzzle.

The expert system is a perfect example of symbolic AI in action. Think of the expert system as a high-level virtual consultant in a specific field - be it medicine, finance or engineering. To dispense its advice, it relies on a manually coded knowledge base and clearly defined inference rules.

Take for example, in the medical field, an expert system that could be fed by a detailed knowledge base on diseases, their symptoms, causes and treatments. If a patient enters a series of symptoms, the system can scan its knowledge base to identify the disease that best corresponds to these symptoms, and suggest an appropriate treatment.

Symbolic AI also paved the way for the first attempts at natural language processing (NLP). These systems attempted to understand and generate language using formal grammar and semantic rules. ELIZA was one of the first NLP programs, developed in the 1960s. ELIZA used rules to simulate a conversation by analyzing user input and generating appropriate responses. However, ELIZA and other early NLP systems had significant limitations. They often struggled to cope with the ambiguity, variety and complexity of natural language.

Despite this, symbolic artificial intelligence has played a fundamental role in the history of AI. It laid the foundations for knowledge representation and problem solving in systems. Even though modern deep learning methods have surpassed symbolic AI in many areas, such as NLP, understanding and appreciating symbolic AI remains essential to understanding the development and potential of artificial intelligence.

The Rise of Machine Learning:

Machine learning, a key sub-discipline of artificial intelligence, has evolved dramatically over the years, offering an ever-wider range of powerful tools for data-driven analysis and prediction. The progression of this technology has been marked by the evolution of diverse methods, from simple decision trees to sophisticated Support Vector Machines (SVMs). By tracing this journey, we can understand how machine learning has moved from mimicking human decision-making to manipulating multidimensional spaces for complex classification tasks.

The first stage of our journey takes us to the discovery of decision trees. These simple but effective graphical structures mimic human decision-making logic. By dividing data into smaller subsets, or "branches", they traverse a series of questions to reach a conclusion, or "leaf", which represents a decision.

Let's take the example of bank credit allocation. Banks can use a decision tree to assess the creditworthiness of a credit applicant. Variables such as income, employment, age and credit history form the branches of the tree, ultimately leading to a decision: to approve or reject the credit application. Despite their ease of use and interpretation, decision trees have their limitations. They tend to overfit training data, i.e. they can become too complex and lose their ability to generalize from new data.

Beyond decision trees, our journey takes us to Support Vector Machines (SVMs). These sophisticated algorithms seek to find the optimal hyperplane for separating classes in a multi-dimensional feature space. Imagine a set of points colored red and blue on a plane. The objective of the SVM is to find a line that best separates the red points from the blue points. As an example, SVMs can be used to classify e-mails as "spam" or "non-spam". By taking into account hundreds or even thousands of characteristics (such as the frequency of certain words or the number of links included), they are able to draw a complex boundary that can accurately separate these two categories. SVMs can be difficult to calibrate and adapt to large quantities of data. What's more, unlike decision trees, they are not intuitive to understand or explain.

The advent of deep learning:

Deep learning, a sub-discipline of machine learning, has transformed the field of AI over the past decade. Inspired by the structure and function of the human brain, deep learning uses artificial neural networks with many ("deep") layers to learn hierarchical representations of data.

Convolutional neural networks (CNNs) have revolutionized image recognition, automatically extracting hierarchical spatial features from images through convolution and pooling layers. CNNs are now at the heart of many applications, from facial recognition to object detection in autonomous cars.

Similarly, recurrent neural networks (RNNs) have been a major breakthrough for natural language processing and other tasks involving sequences of data. RNNs have the unique ability to take temporal context into account, retaining a "memory" of previous information in the sequence. However, they can be difficult to train efficiently, leading to the emergence of more stable and efficient variants, such as LSTMs (Long Short-Term Memory) and GRUs (Gated Recurrent Units).

The evolution of AI has seen a shift from rule-based systems to sophisticated deep learning techniques, paving the way for a growing range of applications and impressive advances in tasks once considered the exclusive preserve of humans. However, each stage of this evolution has brought its own challenges and opportunities, and there is still much to discover in this fascinating exploration of the imitation and enhancement of human intelligence.

Moore's Law: driving technological innovation

Moore's Law, named after its author Gordon Moore, co-founder of Intel, is an empirical principle that has had a profound impact on the semiconductor industry and, more broadly, on the entire world of technology. First enunciated in 1965, Moore's Law stipulates that the number of transistors on a microprocessor - which determines its computing power - would double approximately every two years, while maintaining a stable cost. This prediction proved surprisingly accurate over several decades, guiding the rapid evolution of information and communication technologies. It also created an expectation of exponential growth in technology, fuelling constant innovation.

Moore's Law is not, however, a physical law. Rather, it is a self-referential guide for the industry, a kind of self-fulfilling prophecy. Semiconductor manufacturers have planned their R&D efforts around this prediction, striving to double transistor density every two years. It has been a key driver in the evolution of personal computers, the Internet, smartphones and other digital technologies we use today. It has enabled the miniaturization of electronic devices, making it possible to create powerful portable devices. However, as transistors reach sizes close to atomic limits, engineers face significant technical and physical challenges, slowing the rate of progress of Moore's Law. Issues such as power consumption, heat dissipation and quantum effects become more problematic when transistors are miniaturized to this scale.

To keep innovating, the industry is exploring new processor architectures, new manufacturing techniques, and other approaches such as quantum computing. While this law itself may be slowing down, the underlying principle of rapid technological innovation and continuous growth in computing power is more alive than ever.

Moore's Law has profoundly shaped our technological world, and understanding its impact and implications is essential to grasping the evolution and future of information technology. As we enter an era where AI and related technologies play an increasingly important role, it's more relevant than ever to think about what exponential growth in computing power means, and how it can continue to transform our society.

The transition to natural language processing

The revolution in natural language processing (NLP) began in the 1960s with the appearance of the first computer programs designed to interact with humans in natural language. Among them, ELIZA and Parry are particularly noteworthy.

ELIZA, developed by Joseph Weizenbaum at MIT in 1966, is often considered the first chatbot program. It mimicked a Rogerian psychotherapist (clinical interview) by asking open-ended questions and rephrasing the user's statements, giving the illusion of a genuine exchange.

In 1972, Parry made its appearance, created by Stanford University psychiatrist and computer scientist Kenneth Colby. It was a new breakthrough that captivated the scientific community: a computer program called Parry. Created by psychiatrist and computer scientist Kenneth Colby, Parry has opened up new horizons for machine-human conversation, deepening our understanding of the complexity of human intelligence and its simulation in machines.

Parry was unlike anything that had gone before. Instead of drawing on the average intelligence of a human, Colby chose to represent a specific character: a patient suffering from paranoid schizophrenia. Colby's choice was bold and innovative. He used his knowledge of psychiatry to create a convincing simulation of the mentality of a mentally ill person, offering a new perspective on how artificial intelligence could be used to simulate specific human behaviors.

Parry quickly caught the attention of researchers. The program was tested in a series of interactive conversations where psychiatrists, unsure whether they were communicating with a human patient or a computer program, attempted to diagnose Parry. These "interrogations" took place using a technology called ARPANET, a precursor of the Internet as we know it today.

Parry's ability to simulate a realistic conversation impressed many observers. His behavior was so convincing that some psychiatrists were unable to distinguish Parry from a real human patient. These results highlighted the potential of artificial intelligence to simulate complex human behavior and stimulated research into conversational agents, which have become an essential component of modern AI.

Today, Parry is often compared to another AI pioneer, ELIZA, created by Joseph Weizenbaum. While ELIZA was designed to simulate a psychotherapist, Parry was a patient. Both programs played an important role in defining the early frontiers of conversational artificial intelligence.

Although he was born in the 1970s, Parry's legacy lives on. The advances he introduced continue to inspire developments in the field of artificial intelligence. He was also instrumental in showing how the intelligent machine could be used to understand and simulate human mental conditions, paving the way for the use of AI in mental health and psychological research. Designed to simulate a patient with paranoid schizophrenia, Parry presented a more complex approach than ELIZA, including a model of the world and emotion behaviors.

The progression of NLP

Natural Language Processing (NLP) is a fascinating technology that has evolved rapidly and remarkably over the years. From its humble rule-based beginnings to the incredible flexibility and power of today's machine learning-based models, the history of NLP is an illustration of human progress, innovation and the aspiration for a deeper understanding of our world and ourselves. Let's dive in.

Originally, NLP was based on a highly regulated approach. Imagine a system with a strict set of grammatical and syntactic rules for analyzing and generating language. Every sentence, every word, every punctuation mark had to correspond to a precise rule in order to be correctly interpreted. Let's take a concrete example and suppose we wanted to build a system to understand and answer a simple question, such as "What time is it?". With a rule-based approach, we would program the system to recognize the word "time", associate the question with an action (getting the current time), and generate an appropriate answer. However, this approach proved rigid and limited.

What if the question were slightly different, like "Can you tell me the time?" or "What time is it?"? Without a precise rule for these variants, the system would be lost. And that's without taking into account linguistic subtleties, regional dialects, technical jargon, slang and neologisms - all aspects of language that these rule-based systems struggle to handle. We can draw a parallel with most people who have been diagnosed as Autistic, because if you ask the question "Can you tell me the time?", phrased like that the answer will probably be "Yes I can", but that wasn't the intended result of asking the question.

With the advent of machine learning in the 1980s and 1990s, the field of NLP underwent a revolution. Instead of relying on rigid rules, researchers began to train statistical models on vast corpora of text. These models, like children learning their mother tongue, are able to "understand" and reproduce language patterns by absorbing thousands, even millions, of sentences. They adapt to variations, learn new words and expressions, and can even generate text that sounds almost human.

To return to our previous example, a machine learning-based NLP system could correctly answer all variations of the question about the time, because it had learned to recognize the underlying concept (asking for the time) beyond the specific formulations. This evolution enabled a significant leap forward in NLP performance. Tasks once considered extremely complex, such as machine translation, speech recognition and text generation, are now routinely performed by these machine learning-based models.

However, like the rule-based approach, the machine learning approach also has its own challenges and limitations.

Innovative language models: from Word2Vec to BERT and GPT

Over the last few decades, language models have become increasingly sophisticated. In 2013, a decisive step was taken with the introduction of Word2Vec, a model that uses a neural network to learn vector representations of words. To explain this concept, let's imagine the word "king".

In the Word2Vec model, this word is represented by a vector in a multidimensional space. Similar or contextually related words, such as "queen" or "crown", are found close together in this vector space.

As a result, this model has revealed semantic and syntactic relationships between words in impressive ways. For example, using Word2Vec, if you take the vector for "king", subtract "man" and add "woman", you get close to the vector for "queen". This illustrates how Word2Vec captures the relationships between words in a way that previous models couldn't.

Five years after Word2Vec, Google introduced BERT (Bidirectional Encoder Representations from Transformers). Whereas previous models examined the context of a word based on the words preceding it in a sentence, BERT introduced a major innovation by examining the context of words in both directions, both before and after the word.

This gave BERT a more precise understanding of language. To illustrate this, let's take the example of the sentence "He took the dog out of the bag". An earlier model might misinterpret this sentence as a person taking a literal dog out of a bag. BERT, on the other hand, looking at the context of the words in both directions, can understand that "taking the dog out of the bag" is a figurative expression meaning to reveal a secret. This brings us to OpenAI's GPT (Generative Pre-Training Transformer) series of models, with ChatGPT as a notable example.

GPT models use an attention mechanism called Transformer to generate text in a convincing way. To understand this concept, consider the task of translating a sentence from English to French. A model like OpenAI's will examine each word and its context to produce the appropriate translation. But what really sets GPT apart is its ability to generate text that resembles that written by a human. If you ask ChatGPT to write a story about a trip into space, it can produce a complex and convincing narrative that sounds like it was written by a real person.

These advances, from Word2Vec to ChatGPT, laid the foundations for the rapid evolution of NLP and conversational AI that we see today. They have opened up new possibilities for human-machine interaction and automation. The potential of these technologies is enormous, and they will continue to shape our future in profound and unpredictable ways. These advances, from Eliza to ChatGPT, have laid the foundations for the rapid evolution of NLP and conversational AI we see today. The next step is to explore what these technologies mean for our future.

The language model revolution with OpenAI:

Language models are a sub-discipline of artificial intelligence, focusing on the creation of systems capable of understanding and generating text in a natural way. While early language models were basic and limited in their ability to generate text fluently, the introduction of the GPT (Generative Pre-Training Transformer) series by OpenAI marked a revolution in the field, leading to the birth of ChatGPT, a powerful and versatile language model.

The first GPT model was introduced in 2018, marking a turning point in the field of NLP (Natural Language Processing). These models are based on an architecture called "Transformer", which uses an attention mechanism to weight the relative importance of words in a text. This enables GPT models to understand the context and nuances of human language at a much deeper level than their predecessors.

The pre-training approach used by GPT involves "pre-training" the model on a large amount of text, then training it specifically on a given task. This allows GPT to learn a rich, nuanced representation of human language before being refined for specific tasks. This pre-training process has been a key factor in the success of GPT models.

From GPT to GPT-3: The evolution of language models

Since the introduction of the first GPT model, the series has undergone several iterations, each bringing significant improvements in terms of generated text quality and language comprehension. GPT-2, for example, saw a significant increase in model size, enabling better text generation.

However, it was GPT-3, the third iteration in the series, that really turned the NLP field on its head. With 175 billion parameters, GPT-3 is capable of generating text of a quality that is often indistinguishable from that written by a human. Its ability to understand context and generate appropriate responses to a wide range of prompts has opened up new possibilities for the use of language models in real-world applications.

The birth of ChatGPT: A turning point in language models

ChatGPT, a specialized version of GPT-3, has been developed specifically to generate conversational responses. While previous versions of GPT were already capable of generating text, ChatGPT is unique in that it has been trained specifically on conversational data, enabling it to generate more natural, fluid responses in a conversational context.

ChatGPT was trained using a mix of human supervision and self-learning methods, enabling it to learn from real human conversations. It was then refined to generate responses that were not only grammatically correct, but also relevant and consistent with the context of the conversation.

The emergence of GPT and the subsequent development of ChatGPT marked a veritable revolution in the field of NLP. These advanced language models are capable of generating text of unprecedented quality and consistency, paving the way for new applications and opportunities in the world of AI.

The GPT-4 revolution and plug-ins: a bold step forward

Since GPT-3, the advances have been breathtaking, leading to the emergence of GPT-4, currently the most advanced language model. GPT-4 boasts an incredible number of parameters, far surpassing its predecessors. This increase in size has further enhanced the quality of the generated text, making it almost indistinguishable from that written by a human.

What really sets GPT-4 apart is its flexibility and adaptability, thanks to the introduction of plugins. These plugins are programmable extensions that add extra functionality to the basic model. For example, a plugin can be designed to specialize in text translation, enabling GPT-4 to translate languages with unprecedented accuracy. Another plugin can help GPT-4 understand and generate legal texts, making the model useful in the legal field.

Take, for example, a lawyer working on a complex case. Using GPT-4 with the legal plugin, the lawyer can request an overview of relevant laws, get a summary of similar previous cases, and even get help drafting legal documents. The answers generated are not only grammatically correct, but also accurate, relevant and rich in information.

In the field of education, a teacher could use a dedicated plugin to generate personalized quiz questions for his students. By simply entering the subject and difficulty level, GPT-4 could produce quality questions, helping to reinforce student learning.

GPT-4's plug-in architecture has made possible an almost infinite number of applications. It has enabled the technology to be truly customizable and adaptable to users' specific needs. Thanks to this major breakthrough, we have entered a new era of conversational AI, where limits are constantly being pushed back and new possibilities are constantly being discovered.

The Emergence of ChatGPT: A turning point in AI

The OpenAI story

OpenAI is a San Francisco-based artificial intelligence research organization founded in December 2015 by a group of leading technologists and entrepreneurs, including Elon Musk, Sam Altman, Greg Brockman, Ilya Sutskever, John Schulman and Wojciech Zaremba. The main aim of this organization is to promote and develop user-friendly AI that benefits all humans.

For the founding company, artificial intelligence is not simply a business technology, but a powerful tool that can solve many of our society's challenges, from health problems to environmental issues. With a firm commitment to the principles of transparency and cooperation, OpenAI works to create AI systems that are not only technologically advanced, but also ethically responsible.

OpenAI's impact on the field of artificial intelligence has been significant. The organization's research has helped advance our understanding of artificial intelligence, and its language models, such as GPT-4 and ChatGPT, have revolutionized the way we interact with AI.

Using deep learning to create ChatGPT

ChatGPT's underlying architecture is based on a machine learning model called Transformer, which was introduced by Vaswani et al. in 2017. Transformer is based on deep neural networks, which are AI systems inspired by the workings of the human brain.

To train ChatGPT, OpenAI used a technique known as deep learning, which involves training neural networks on large quantities of data. In the case of ChatGPT, this data consisted of text from the Internet. During training, ChatGPT learns to predict the next word in a sentence based on all previous words, enabling it to generate coherent, sensible responses to user prompts.

The inspiration and motivation behind the creation of ChatGPT

The idea of creating a language model like ChatGPT was largely inspired by the perceived potential of AI to transform the way we communicate and interact with technology. Observing the limitations of existing chat systems, which were often rigid and unable to understand context, the OpenAI team was motivated to develop a system that could understand and respond to prompts in a more natural and conversational way.

Another motivating factor was the idea of paving the way for new applications of artificial intelligence. By developing a language model capable of generating creative texts, OpenAI not only created a useful tool for chat applications, but also opened up new possibilities in fields such as automatic writing, online tutoring and more.

Creating ChatGPT has been an exciting process, guided by OpenAI's mission to advance artificial intelligence for the benefit of all. The result is a tool that redefines how we interact with AI and opens the door to new possibilities for the future.

The technology behind ChatGPT

Transformers and unsupervised learning.

In the dynamic and constantly evolving world of artificial intelligence, two key concepts have played a major role in the transformation of language models: Transformers and Unsupervised Learning. Understanding these concepts is not only interesting from a theoretical point of view, but can also help us appreciate the revolutionary potential of AI-based language models such as ChatGPT.

Transformers have revolutionized the field of natural language processing (NLP) since their introduction in 2017.

But what exactly is a Transformer? Imagine you're trying to understand the meaning of a sentence. You don't read each word individually, do you? Instead, you read the sentence as a whole, taking into account the overall context. This is exactly what Transformers do. They are able to analyze sentences taking into account the whole context, not word by word.

With a simple sentence like "He went to Paris. He loved it." In this case, the "He" in the second sentence refers to the person mentioned in the first sentence. A Transformer-based language model is able to understand this contextual reference, enabling it to generate more coherent and natural responses. This ability to understand the overall context is one of the factors that makes language models like ChatGPT so impressive.

Then there's Unsupervised Learning. In most forms of machine learning, we need to provide labeled data to train a model. For example, to train a model to recognize images of dogs, we would need to provide it with images labeled as "dog" and "not a dog". However, Unsupervised Learning is different. In this case, the model learns by observing and analyzing the data without any labels.

In the case of models like LLAMA or BARD, for example, Unsupervised Learning is used to enable the model to learn from vast quantities of text. The model examines the text, learning patterns, sentence structures and even subtle nuances of meaning, all without any direct human intervention. Imagine an avid librarian devouring thousands of books, learning from every sentence and word, and you'll get an idea of what these models do in their training sessions.

By combining Transformers and Unsupervised Learning, AI language models have opened the door to previously unimaginable applications. Whether it's copywriting, machine translation, automated customer support, or even the creation of poetry and art, these models are redefining what's possible with AI.

By understanding these concepts, we can not only appreciate the sophistication and power of these technologies, but also begin to envision how they might shape our future.

Transformative neural networks: a revolution in AI

Since transformers were introduced in the paper "Attention is All You Need" by Vaswani et al. in 2017, they have revolutionized the field of machine learning, particularly in natural language processing.

Transformer neural networks rely on an attention mechanism that allows the model to focus on different parts of an input sequence when generating an output. Unlike previous models such as recurrent neural networks (RNNs) and LSTMs, transformers do not need to process input sequences in order, enabling them to learn long-term dependencies and parallelize learning more efficiently.

The core of the transformer is the multi-headed attention mechanism that enables the model to capture different types of relationships in the data. Each "head" of attention focuses on a different aspect of the input information, enabling a richer, more nuanced understanding.

Unsupervised learning: ChatGPT's approach to understanding language

At the heart of ChatGPT's technology lies a subtle, sometimes confusing, yet powerful mechanism: unsupervised learning. To grasp the importance of this approach and understand its essential role in ChatGPT's operation, it is necessary to compare it with its counterpart, supervised learning.

Supervised learning is comparable to a dedicated teacher meticulously guiding his or her students through each step of a lesson. The model, in this case, is the student, and each piece of data in the learning set is a separate lesson. Each lesson has a precise objective, or label, that clearly indicates what the student should learn. If we think of the student as a weather prediction model, each label could be a correct prediction of the weather for a specific day.

Unsupervised learning, however, is a different story. It's more like an inquisitive student let loose in an unguided library, with the sole task of spotting patterns, structures and themes in the books he encounters. There are no specific labels or objectives; the student has to find meaning in the data for himself. Herein lies the magic of unsupervised learning: the model is able to discover intrinsic patterns in the data without anyone explicitly telling it what to look for.

Imagine, for example, an unsupervised model trained on thousands of cooking recipes. Without anyone explicitly telling it what a dessert or a main course is, the model could end up grouping the recipes according to certain common characteristics, thus implicitly discovering the notion of "dessert" and "main course". This is exactly the kind of learning process ChatGPT employs.

This conversational model is trained on a vast amount of text from the Internet. It examines every word, every sentence, every paragraph, learning the subtleties and complexities of language as it goes. Like the student in the library, this model has no labels to guide it; it simply learns to predict the next word in a sentence based on context.

However, once this model has assimilated a sufficient amount of data, it is refined using a technique called "Proximal Policy Optimization". It's a bit like our student, having explored the library on his own, meeting a mentor who gives him advice and guidance based on his autonomous learning. This mentor is actually a team of human evaluators who guide this model to improve its performance.

By combining these approaches, ChatGPT is able to understand and generate language with astonishing fluency and naturalness. This is a real feat in the field of artificial intelligence, and an impressive demonstration of the power of unsupervised learning.

Technical details: from data pre-processing to model training

Before being fed into the model, the textual data is pre-processed using a technique called "tokenization", which breaks down the text into smaller units, usually words or sub-words. The conversational model uses a specific tokenization algorithm that takes into account the distribution of words in the training corpus. Once the data has been pre-processed, it is fed into the model for training. The model is trained to predict the next word in a sequence of words, based on all previous words in the sequence. During training, model parameters are adjusted to minimize the difference between model predictions and actual words.

After initial training, the model is refined on a specific set of data under the supervision of human evaluators, to align its responses with human expectations.

The technology behind ChatGPT is complex, but the fundamental principles are based on powerful and intuitive ideas. Transformers and unsupervised learning enable this model to interpret human language with remarkable accuracy and flexibility, paving the way for increasingly sophisticated and useful AI applications.

ChatGPT's involvement in our company:

In our exploration of artificial intelligence, we saw how ChatGPT and its peers have reshaped our understanding of what is technically possible. However, their impact goes far beyond the technology itself. To truly understand the scale of this revolution, it's essential to examine ChatGPT's interaction with our society - the applications, ethical dilemmas and social impact of this surprising language model.

ChatGPT applications :

The conversational model began as a laboratory exercise, a technical challenge to create a machine capable of generating plausible human text. We're a long way from the fears generated by James Cameron's sci-fi films when it comes to the future of artificial intelligence. The aim is simply to be able to interact easily with a conversational tool. However, since its creation, it has become clear that its potential applications are wide and varied.

In the field of copywriting, for example, ChatGPT has become an invaluable tool. Writers use AI to generate ideas, create drafts and even polish their prose. Journalists use it to write reports, marketers to create compelling content, and teachers to create educational material. It's not about replacing humans, but rather assisting them, making these tasks less laborious and more efficient. This is also the case for yours truly, who uses these tools to develop ideas and make them more readable. For example, you can ask him to explain a complicated concept like quantum computing to an 8-year-old child, because he does it very well.

Beyond editorial, ChatGPT has found a place in the world of customer service. Able to understand user queries and generate useful answers, it has become a first line of support for many companies. It helps solve common problems and guides users towards solutions, leaving humans to deal with more complex cases. Major companies such as IBM are planning to replace around 7,800 positions, or 30% of their support functions, with artificial intelligence over the next 5 years. This decision will not result in redundancies, but in a hiring freeze and unreplaced departures. A recent Goldman Sachs report estimates that technologies like ChatGPT could affect up to 300 million jobs worldwide, with a quarter of those jobs eventually eliminated. However, AI could also boost productivity and global GDP by 7% by automating certain tasks.

Understanding challenges and solutions :

However, as we embrace these new applications, we must also confront new ethical challenges. Language models like ChatGPT are capable of generating text that sounds human, but they have no understanding or awareness of what they are saying. This can lead to situations where AI produces inappropriate, misleading or offensive content.

This is where ethical principles come into play. The designers of these systems are working tirelessly to find ways of limiting these potential abuses. This includes techniques to filter out inappropriate content, to give users greater control over AI responses, and to ensure full transparency about the limits and capabilities of these systems.

AI for the common good:

Beyond individual questions of use and ethics, there is the wider impact of conversational models on society. The intelligent machine has the potential to improve the lives of many people, but it can also be a source of division and conflict.

Here are a few examples of applications with their advantages and disadvantages:

Education: artificial intelligence, including conversational models, can be used to create personalized learning assistants. These assistants can help students understand complex concepts, offer extra support outside class hours and provide personalized learning paths. However, this can also widen the digital divide, as access to these technologies is not evenly distributed.

Health: Health chatbots can provide basic medical advice and help manage chronic diseases. They can improve healthcare accessibility, especially in remote areas. Nevertheless, this could lead to the dehumanization of healthcare and data privacy issues.

Employment: artificial intelligence can automate certain repetitive tasks, freeing up workers' time. For example, ChatGPT can be used to automate answers to frequently asked customer service questions. However, this could also lead to job losses, particularly for low-skilled workers.

Social media and fake news: Conversational models can be used to generate online content in large quantities, which can contribute to misinformation and fake news. They can also be used to generate hate speech or offensive content, which can exacerbate social conflict.

Justice and fairness: artificial intelligence can be made accessible to all to better inform people about their rights and relieve court congestion, but if conversational models are used for applications such as recruitment or credit decisions, they could reinforce existing biases in these processes if the training data is biased.

Privacy and surveillance: Artificial intelligence can be used to monitor people's conversations and behavior and greatly improve security, but this also raises important questions about privacy and consent.

Technological dependence: If people start to rely heavily on AI for communication, this could lead to a degradation of human communication skills and increased isolation. Here, too, we need to keep in mind that it's a great help, but that human contact and learning also need to be maintained.

The ultimate goal is to ensure that artificial intelligence is used for the common good. This means making it accessible to all, not just those who can afford to use it. It also means using it to address societal challenges, from education to health to the environment.

It's an ambitious goal, but as artificial intelligence becomes increasingly ubiquitous, it's essential that we strive to achieve it. Learning how to use it well, and helping to steer its development in the right direction, also means avoiding a certain kind of obscurantism on the subject, and leaving it to an ill-intentioned caste who will take advantage of some people's ignorance.

It's clear that ChatGPT's impact goes far beyond the technology itself. Its implication for our society is profound, touching everything from the way we work to the way we interact with the world. As we continue to explore the possibilities of AI, it's important that we do so with constant attention to the ethical and social implications of our work.

The Future of AI

Artificial intelligence, with language models such as ChatGPT, LLAMA , CLAUDE or BARD at its prow, continues to progress at a breakneck pace. A few decades ago, most of the ideas we now associate with AI were truly the stuff of science fiction. Today, they are increasingly shaping our lives in tangible ways, profoundly transforming diverse sectors from medicine to finance, education to the entertainment industry. As we look to the future, it's worth considering what we can expect from the next generation of AI and conversational models.

A major challenge for future language models is to improve their understanding of context. Currently, although these models are good at generating text based on the training data they have received, they may still struggle to grasp the subtle context in which a conversation takes place. For example, if a user asks an ambiguous question such as "Where is he?", a conversational model might struggle to give a precise answer, as the question depends heavily on the context of the previous conversation.

But with spectacular advances in machine learning algorithms and innovative approaches to context encoding (not to mention ever-increasing computing power), we can expect to see significant improvements in this area. We could envisage future language models using advanced natural language processing techniques to interpret the meaning of sentences in the context of a wider conversation, or even on the basis of past interactions with a specific user. Improved model training will make them more efficient, and so will technological advances.

Personalization is another key area for improvement. Currently, most language models are trained on general data and do not take into account individual specificities. However, in the near future, we could see versions of ChatGPT that are able to adapt to the language preferences, interaction styles and even specific interests of each user. To illustrate this, imagine a ChatGPT that remembers your favorite reading material, adapts its writing style to your preferences and can even recommend new reading material based on your tastes.

In the continuing evolution of AI, several areas promise to further transform the way we interact with these technologies. Among these, explanatory AI and real-time AI are particularly noteworthy.

Explanatory AI aims to make artificial intelligence processes more transparent and understandable to humans. Today, language models like ChatGPT are often seen as "black boxes". We give them a prompt, they generate a response, but the precise process they use to produce that response is often opaque. With the explanatory intelligent machine, it might be possible to ask a language model not only to produce a response, but also to explain how and why it produced that specific response. For example, in a teaching context, an explanatory language model could not only solve a math problem, but also detail the steps it took to arrive at the solution.

When it comes to real-time AI, most interactions with language models are currently via static text - we provide a prompt, wait for a response, then provide another prompt. However, as technology advances, we could see an increase in real-time AI applications, where the language model interacts with users in real time, generating responses based on real-time input. This could enable more fluid and natural conversations with artificial intelligence, which could, for example, be used to simulate live exchanges with human experts in various fields, from health advisors to academic tutors.

Emotional intelligent machine, also known as artificial emotional intelligence, refers to the ability of AI systems to recognize, interpret and respond appropriately to human emotions. While current interactions with artificial intelligence are mainly focused on information exchange, emotional AI could enable a new dimension of interaction, where artificial intelligence is able to understand and react to the user's moods, feelings and emotional intentions. This capability could be particularly useful in fields such as customer service, where empathy and emotional understanding are key, or in mental health applications, where artificial intelligence could help provide emotional support to users.

At the same time, general artificial intelligence, also known as AGI (Artificial General Intelligence), represents a major ambition in the field of AI. Whereas current AI systems, including language models such as ChatGPT, are specialized and designed to accomplish specific tasks, AGI would refer to an intelligent machine system capable of understanding, learning and applying its knowledge to a wide variety of tasks, in the same way that a human can. AGI is often seen as the holy grail of AI research, but its realization poses many technical and ethical challenges. Nevertheless, its potential to transform the way we interact with technology is undeniable.

Each evolution in artificial intelligence brings with it new possibilities, but also new challenges and concerns. It is necessary to bear in mind that the development of artificial intelligence must be guided by ethical considerations and standards of responsibility to ensure that these technologies are used in a way that benefits everyone, while minimizing potential risks. Ultimately, the future of AI depends on our ability to navigate these complexities and balance technological advances with respect for our fundamental values.

The importance of models like ChatGPT for the future of AI

ChatGPT is not only a useful tool for today (there are many others); it also sets the scene for the future of AI. Understanding how to interact with a conversational model, how it works, and how we can get the most out of it, means preparing for a world in which artificial intelligence will play an even more central role.

As a training tool, this language model can help users familiarize themselves with the language of AI, understand how to structure their queries for optimal results, and discover new ways of using AI to solve problems. As a catalyst for creativity, this conversational model can help stimulate new ideas, explore hypothetical scenarios and generate new perspectives. And as a precursor to the future of AI, ChatGPT offers valuable insight into the challenges and opportunities we can expect as AI continues to evolve and develop.

The precise direction the future of ChatGPT or any other model and AI in general will take remains to be seen. But what is certain is that this technology continues to advance at a rapid pace, promising significant transformations in the way we live, work and interact with the world around us. As individuals, as companies, it's vital that we are ready to navigate this new horizon with wisdom, curiosity and an open mind.

-2-

Language models

"AI will help us free humanity from repetitive tasks."

Kai-Fu Lee

Understanding Machine Learning

Machine Learning is a branch of artificial intelligence that focuses on the development of systems capable of learning and improving their performance from data, without being explicitly programmed to do so. It's the art of teaching computers to do what humans do naturally: learn from experience. To do this, machine learning uses algorithms to find patterns in the data, then apply these patterns to perform various tasks, such as prediction, classification, clustering, and generating new data. It is the driving force behind many modern technologies, from speech and visual recognition to machine translation and the recommendation systems used by streaming and e-commerce platforms.

There are three main types of machine learning: supervised learning, unsupervised learning and reinforcement learning.

Supervised learning is the most common form. In this framework, the algorithm learns from a set of labeled training data, where each example is associated with a correct answer. The aim is to build a model capable of predicting the correct answer for new examples, based on the characteristics of these examples. Classification problems (e.g., determining whether an e-mail is spam or not) and regression problems (e.g., predicting the price of a house based on its characteristics) are usually addressed with supervised learning.

Imagine a classroom, where a skilled teacher guides his students through a series of lessons. For example, he might show them several pictures of animals - a cat, a dog, a bird, a fish - and label each picture with the name of the corresponding animal. In this way, students learn to associate the picture with the correct animal. When the teacher then shows them a new picture of an animal they've already seen, they can correctly identify it thanks to the previous lessons.

This situation is an example of supervised learning, where the teacher is the Machine Learning algorithm, and the students are the models being trained. In supervised learning, we have input data - images of animals - which are associated with output labels - the names of the animals. The supervised learning algorithm uses this training data to learn a model that can correctly associate the new input data with the correct output label.

Let's take a more concrete example of the application of supervised learning in finance. Suppose a bank wants to predict whether a customer is likely to repay a loan or not. To do this, it can use a set of historical data on its customers, containing information such as age, income, employment, credit history, etc., as well as information on whether the customer has repaid the loan or defaulted. In this case, customer information is the input and loan repayment information is the output label. A supervised learning algorithm can be trained on this data to learn a model that can predict, for a new customer, whether he is likely to repay the loan or not, based on the patterns it has learned from the historical data.

Thus, supervised learning enables our models to learn from labeled data to make accurate predictions about new data, in the same way that a student learns from a teacher's lessons to answer new questions correctly.

Unsupervised learning, on the other hand, concerns situations where we have data, but no labeled responses. The aim is to discover the hidden structure in the data. Common problems addressed by unsupervised learning include clustering (e.g., segmenting customers into groups based on their purchasing behavior) and dimensionality reduction (e.g., compressing high-dimensional information into a lower-dimensional space while retaining important structures).

This is a machine-learning method in which the model is led to discover the underlying structures and patterns in the data without being told the results beforehand. Imagine a young child entering a room full of toys for the first time. No one has told him what each type of toy looks like or how to classify them. However, after spending some time exploring the room, the child begins to group toys according to their common characteristics: all the teddy bears in one corner, all the toy cars in another, and so on. He may even recognize sub-groups, such as small racing cars on one side and big trucks on the other.

This is the principle of unsupervised learning. For example, let's take a large online store that wants to understand its customers' buying habits so it can offer them more relevant products. They have at their disposal tons of anonymized data on their customers' purchasing history, but this data is unlabeled, i.e. it doesn't specify which customers are similar to each other, or what type of products each customer is likely to buy. By using unsupervised learning techniques, such as clustering, the model can discover groups of customers who buy similar products and use this information to improve product recommendations. For example, if the model discovers that a group of customers regularly buys science fiction books and board games, it could recommend the latest space-themed board game to these customers. Unsupervised learning opens up a vast field of exploration and discovery by enabling AI models to explore complex, unstructured datasets and uncover valuable information. It's like giving an explorer a blank map and letting him discover the mountains, valleys and rivers on his own. The results can sometimes be surprising, leading to discoveries we'd never have thought to look for if we'd limited ourselves to supervised learning approaches.

Reinforcement learning is a more complex approach where an agent learns to perform actions in an environment in order to maximize a certain reward. It is commonly used in domains such as gaming, robotics and navigation, where the objective is to learn a series of actions that lead to the final goal.

It's an approach to machine learning where an agent, which is typically a computer program, learns how to behave in an environment by performing certain actions and receiving rewards or punishments in return. To help you understand this, imagine a maze game where the objective is to find a hidden treasure. In this context, the agent would be a small digital creature that is placed somewhere in the maze and has to find its way to the treasure.

At first, the creature has no idea which way to go. So he begins to explore the labyrinth at random. Sometimes it comes up against a wall (which could be considered a punishment), or sometimes it finds a small amount of gold (which could be considered a reward). As he explores, the creature begins to understand the labyrinth. He learns, for example, that there's always a wall in a certain direction, or that gold is always found near a certain landmark. It also learns to avoid punishment (i.e., bumping into walls) and to look for rewards (i.e., gold).

Over time, through this trial-and-error approach, and by taking advantage of rewards and punishments, the creature learns to navigate the maze efficiently to find the treasure. This is essentially what happens in reinforcement learning. An agent explores its environment, learning actions that lead to positive rewards and avoiding those that lead to negative rewards, in order to achieve a specific goal. This learning method has proved effective in a variety of fields, from games and robotics to logistics and route planning.

The role of data :

Data is the fuel of Machine Learning models, like the coal that powers the locomotive of a steam train, or the gasoline that makes a car engine roar. Without data, algorithms don't have the raw material they need to learn, evolve and adapt. To illustrate this point, imagine a child learning to recognize the different species of birds. At first, he can't tell a chickadee from a robin. But, with time and repeated observation of different species, he begins to recognize their distinctive features: the vibrant color of a robin's breast, the small size and blue and yellow plumage of a chickadee. Each observation enriches his learning curve and sharpens his ability to distinguish between different bird species.

In the same way, a Machine Learning algorithm needs data to learn. Let's take the example of an image recognition algorithm. It is provided with thousands, even millions of images of birds, each labelled with the species of bird represented. The algorithm trains itself by analyzing these images, learning to recognize the characteristics that define each species. Given enough data and time to learn, the algorithm becomes capable of distinguishing a chickadee from a robin with impressive accuracy.

But it's not just about having lots of data. The quality of the data is just as important. If the algorithm is trained on mislabeled images, or on a dataset that doesn't properly represent the diversity of bird species, it won't be able to make accurate predictions in the real world. It's as if a child learns to recognize birds by looking only at cartoon images of birds, rather than real photos. The quality of his learning would be greatly affected.

In short, data is essential for Machine Learning, both in terms of quantity and quality. It enables algorithms to learn, adapt and evolve, just as observation and experience enable a child to learn to recognize different species of birds. Data is the fuel that powers the machine learning engine, enabling these algorithms to transform raw piles of information into valuable knowledge and predictions.

In short, machine learning is a dynamic and constantly evolving field that lies at the heart of many modern technologies. By understanding its fundamental principles, we can better grasp how these systems learn and operate, which is essential to appreciating the potential and challenges of AI.

Deep learning is a sub-category of Machine Learning that uses multi-layered neural networks, or "deep neural networks". These neural networks are inspired by the workings of the human brain, attempting to replicate its model of information processing and pattern creation for decision-making. Deep learning focuses on training algorithms to learn and understand on their own by exposing the model to vast quantities of data. This is essentially how an AI system can "learn" from unstructured, unlabeled data.

For example, let's take the case of image recognition, a field where deep learning has largely surpassed traditional machine learning approaches. By feeding a large number of images of a certain object to a deep neural network (for example, thousands of images of cats), the model can "learn" to identify what constitutes a cat. It does this by identifying common features that occur in all cat images, and then using these features to identify cats in new images it has never seen before. So, if we show the model a new image of a cat that it has never seen before, it can correctly identify that it is a cat based on what it has learned before.

Similarly, in the field of machine translation, deep learning models such as Transformer have radically improved the quality of translations. By learning pairs of sentences in two languages, these models can learn correspondences and grammatical structures, and are able to produce much more accurate and natural translations than traditional approaches.

The advances made thanks to deep learning are not limited to these fields. It is also at the heart of advances in speech synthesis, text generation, voice recognition, and even more complex fields such as autonomous driving, where deep learning is used to interpret sensor data in real time and make driving decisions.

A neural network is made up of numerous units, or neurons, which are organized into layers. There are three types of layer in a neural network: the input layer, the hidden layer(s), and the output layer. Each layer can contain any number of neurons, and each neuron is connected to all the other neurons in the previous and next layers.

The different types of neural networks: from deep learning to backpropagation. There are many different types of neural network, each with its own particularities and applications. Which type of neural network to use depends on the specific task in hand.

Feedforward neural networks are the simplest. Information flows in a single direction, from input to output. They are a type of artificial neural network in which information moves in a single direction: from input to output, without loops or feedback connections. In other words, these networks have no memory of previous inputs - each input is processed independently.

Here's an example to help you understand how they work. Let's imagine a feedforward neural network used for image recognition, for example to determine whether a given image is that of a dog or a cat.

The input image would first be transformed into a set of numerical values corresponding to the color (or intensity) of each pixel. These values would then be fed into the network's first "layer" of neurons. Each neuron in this layer would take a number of these values, multiply them by specific "weights" (which are adjusted as the network learns), and then sum these products. Then, an activation function would be applied to this sum, producing the neuron's "output".

This output is then transmitted to the next layer of neurons, where the process is repeated. By traversing the network in this way, information is progressively transformed from raw input (pixel values) to output (the decision: "dog" or "cat").

A key aspect of feedforward neural networks is that they have no notion of "time" or "sequence". They don't remember previous inputs - each image is processed independently of the others. This distinguishes them from other types of neural networks, such as recurrent neural networks, which have feedforward connections and can thus maintain a kind of "memory" of previous inputs.

Convolutional neural networks (CNNs) are particularly effective for processing images. They use a mathematical operation called convolution to process data hierarchically, enabling them to recognize complex patterns in images. The particularity of these networks lies in their architecture, inspired by the structure of the visual cortex of animals.

Their name comes from the convolution operation, a mathematical operation that combines two functions to produce a third. In the context of CNNs, the convolution operation is used to apply filters to an image in order to detect certain features, such as contours, textures or colors.

To understand how a CNN works, let's imagine an example. Suppose we wanted to train a CNN to recognize images of dogs. We would start by providing the network with a large number of dog images. The network begins by applying filters to these images to detect low-level features, such as lines and curves. These features are then passed on to deeper layers of the network, which combine them to detect higher-level features, such as shapes or patterns. Finally, the deeper layers of the network combine these higher-level features to recognize the overall object - in this case, a dog.

Another practical example of CNNs is in the field of facial recognition. CNNs are able to detect individual facial features, such as eyes, nose and mouth, and then combine these features to recognize a specific face. This is how most modern facial recognition smartphone unlocking systems work.

In short, CNNs are a powerful class of deep learning models that are particularly suited to image processing. Their ability to automatically and hierarchically detect features from input data has enabled them to outperform traditional image processing approaches in many tasks.

Recurrent neural networks (RNN) are designed to process sequential data, such as text or time series. They have the distinctive feature of loop connections, enabling them to retain a "memory" of previously processed information. RNNs are particularly useful when context is important in interpreting data, as in the case of text, speech, time sequences and more.

The main distinguishing feature of an RNN is its internal loop structure, enabling information to be passed from one stage of the sequence to the next. This means that, instead of processing each input independently, an RNN takes previous inputs into account to understand the current input. In other words, RNNs have a kind of "memory".

Let's take a concrete example: suppose we're trying to predict the next word in a sentence, such as "It's a nice day today, I think I'll go out for a _____". A non-recursive model would treat each word individually, disregarding the context provided by the preceding words. So it might predict something like "pizza", which is a common word, but doesn't match the context of the sentence.

An RNN, on the other hand, remembers the previous words ("It's a nice day today, I think I'll go out for one") and uses this context to make a more accurate prediction. Therefore, it might predict the word "walk", which makes much more sense in this context.

Another example would be stock price prediction. RNNs can use share prices from previous days to help predict future prices, taking into account trends and patterns in historical data.

However, traditional RNNs have difficulty handling long-term dependencies due to the gradient fading problem, where the information from the first input becomes increasingly diluted as one progresses through the sequence. To solve this problem, variants of RNNs, such as **LSTM** (Long Short-Term Memory) and **GRU** (Gated Recurrent Unit) networks, have been introduced, which have a better ability to maintain long-term information.

Backpropagation is an efficient learning algorithm used in neural networks. It adjusts the weights of connections in the network according to the error between predicted and actual output. It is this process that enables the neural network to "learn" from the data. The main aim of backpropagation is to minimize the error between model predictions and expected actual values, by progressively adjusting the weights and biases of the network.

Let's imagine a simple example: we have a neural network designed to predict whether or not an image contains a cat. We pass an image through the network, which produces a prediction based on its current weights and biases. For example, the network could wrongly predict that an image of a dog is a cat.

The first step in backpropagation is to calculate the network error, i.e. the difference between the network prediction ("cat") and the actual truth ("dog"). This error is usually calculated using a cost function, such as root mean square error or cross-entropy.

Once the error has been calculated, backpropagation "propagates" this error backwards through the network, from the last layer to the first. At each layer, the algorithm uses gradient calculation to determine the extent to which each weight and bias has contributed to the overall error. In other words, it determines which neurons have "done right" and which have "done wrong".

Finally, the algorithm adjusts the weights and biases of the network to minimize the error. For example, if a particular weight has contributed significantly to the error, that weight will be reduced. Conversely, if a weight has contributed to a correct prediction, that weight will be increased. These adjustments are made using a learning rate, which determines the size of the adjustments.

By repeating this process on numerous training examples (images of cats and dogs in our case), the network learns to distinguish cats from dogs. The weights and biases of the network have adjusted to minimize the error on the training data, and the network is now able to make more accurate predictions on new data it has never seen before. This is the basic principle of backpropagation in neural networks.

The art of machine learning algorithms

Machine learning algorithms are the engine that powers the magic of artificial intelligence. These are the mathematical formulas and computational processes that enable machines to learn from data, make decisions and perform tasks that were once reserved for humans. Algorithms range in complexity from classical techniques such as linear regression to advanced methods such as Support Vector Machines (SVM) and gradient boosting.

Classic algorithms: from linear regression to decision trees

The starting point for any exploration of machine learning algorithms is an understanding of classical techniques. Linear regression, for example, is one of the oldest and simplest. It involves finding a line, plane or hyperplane that best fits a set of data points. It is the technique of choice for numerical prediction where the relationship between inputs and output is approximately linear. Decision trees, on the other hand, are prediction models used in classification and regression problems. They work by creating a decision tree where each node represents a function of the inputs and each leaf represents a prediction value. Decision trees are easy to understand and visualize, making them popular for exploratory data analysis.

To go a step further, linear regression and decision trees are two examples of classic machine learning algorithms that have been widely used in many fields to solve various types of problems. To better understand how they work, let's look at two practical examples.

Let's start with the example of linear regression. Suppose you work for a real estate company and want to predict house prices based on square footage. Using a dataset containing information on previously sold houses, with house area (in square feet) as the input variable and sales price as the output variable, you could train a linear regression model. This model would attempt to find the line that best matches the distribution of data in the area versus price graph. This line, or "line of best fit", can then be used to predict the price of a house based on its square footage. So, if a new 100-square-meter house comes on the market, the model could predict its price by locating the 100-square-meter area on the x-axis, moving up to the regression line, and reading the corresponding price on the y-axis. This is the power of linear regression: with an approximately linear relationship, it's easy to predict a numerical output.

Next, let's take the example of decision trees. Imagine you're a doctor trying to predict whether a patient is at risk of developing a certain disease based on a set of symptoms. Using a decision tree, each node in the tree would represent a question related to a specific symptom - for example, "Does the patient have a fever?", "Does the patient have abdominal pain?" and so on. The branches coming out of each node would represent the possible answers to these questions. By following the branches according to the answers to the questions, you would eventually reach a leaf of the tree, which represents a prediction of the presence or absence of the disease. The decision tree thus facilitates the diagnostic process by formalizing a series of decisions based on observable symptoms. Its visual structure also makes the explanation of predictions more transparent, as it is possible to retrace the path that led to each prediction.

Ensemble methods :

As we progress in complexity, we come across ensemble methods. These techniques combine several machine learning models to improve predictive performance. Bagging, boosting and Random Forest are among the best-known.

Bagging, or Bootstrap Aggregating, creates several subsets of the original data set, builds a model for each subset, then aggregates the results. Boosting, on the other hand, trains a series of models sequentially, with each model seeking to correct the errors of its predecessor. Finally, Random Forest is an ensemble method that uses multiple decision trees to produce a robust prediction.

To better understand these methods, they harness the "wisdom of crowds" by bringing together several simpler models to create a more powerful and robust model. Let's look at a few concrete examples to illustrate how bagging, boosting and random forest work.

Bagging is like a jury in an art competition. Each judge, with his or her own preferences and points of view, evaluates a work of art based on a distinct part of the total work. Their individual judgment may vary, but by combining their opinions, a more global and balanced appreciation of the work is achieved. Similarly, bagging creates several subsets of the original dataset, each driving its own machine learning model. The predictions of all these models are then aggregated, for example by majority vote for classification problems, or by average for regression problems. This approach reduces variance and avoids overlearning, which often leads to better predictive performance.

Boosting, on the other hand, is more like a sports coach working with a team over a series of matches. At first, the team may make several mistakes, but after each match, the coach analyzes the errors and guides the team to correct them in the next match. As the matches progress, the team becomes more and more competent. In the context of machine learning, boosting follows a similar process: it starts with a simple model, identifies its errors, then builds another model that attempts to correct these errors. This process is repeated several times, creating a series of models that learn from each other. Boosting can therefore transform a set of weak models into a powerful one, but it must be used with caution to avoid overlearning.

Finally, the **Random Forest** is like an assembly of wise men deliberating on a subject. Each wise man, with his own set of knowledge and experience, gives his opinion on the matter. By collecting and combining their opinions, the assembly arrives at a well-informed decision. In machine learning, the Random Forest creates a large number of decision trees, each trained on a different subset of the original data set. Each tree makes an independent prediction, and these predictions are then combined to give the final prediction. Random Forest is therefore an ensemble method that offers good predictive performance, resistance to overlearning and the ability to handle a large number of input variables, making it popular in many application fields.

Advanced algorithms: Support Vector Machines and Gradient Boosting

At the frontier of machine learning research are advanced techniques such as Support Vector Machines (SVM) and gradient boosting.

The Support Vector Machine (SVM) is a machine learning algorithm widely used for classification and regression tasks. The basic idea behind SVM is to find a hyperplane or line that best separates the data in a multi-dimensional space. This line is chosen to maximize the margin between different classes of data.

To better understand, imagine you have a set of points on a plane that are either red or blue. The aim of an SVM is to find a line that best separates these two sets of points. This line is chosen so that the distance between the line and the nearest point in each set (red and blue) is maximized. These nearest points are called "support vectors", hence the name "Support Vector Machine".

Sometimes, the data are not linearly separable, i.e. there is no straight line that can perfectly separate them. In such cases, SVM uses a trick called "the kernel trick" to transform the data into a higher dimension where they are separable. For example, if you have two sets of points in a plane that are arranged in concentric circles, you can't draw a straight line to separate them. However, if you transform the data into a higher dimension, for example by adding a third dimension, then you can separate the data with a plane.

Gradient Boosting is a machine learning technique for regression and classification problems, which produces a prediction model in the form of a set of weak prediction models, usually decision trees. The basic idea behind Gradient Boosting is to add new models to the overall model sequentially, with each new model correcting the errors made by the previous overall model.

To illustrate, imagine you're trying to solve a complex puzzle. Your first attempt at solving it may be far from the final solution, but it gives you a starting point. Now, instead of throwing away that first attempt and starting again from scratch, you look at where you made mistakes in your first attempt and try to correct those mistakes in your next attempt. You repeat this process, each new attempt focusing on correcting the mistakes of the previous one, until you have a solution that is close enough to the final one. This is essentially how Gradient Boosting works.

In the context of machine learning, each "attempt" is a weak prediction model (often a decision tree), each "error" is a difference between the current predictions and the actual values, and the "error correction" process is carried out by adjusting the weights of the observations according to the previous errors. In the end, all the weak models are combined to form a more powerful overall model.

The art of machine learning algorithms lies in selecting and applying the right technique to the right problem. Whether classic techniques, ensemble methods or advanced algorithms, each algorithm has its place in the data scientist's toolbox. By understanding the strengths and weaknesses of each algorithm, we can harness the full potential of this exciting technology and transform the way we live and work.

The importance of model evaluation and optimization

It's essential to understand that creating a machine learning model involves much more than simply training an algorithm on a data set. Model evaluation and optimization are crucial aspects of the machine learning process, ensuring that the model we create is robust, reliable and fit for purpose.

Evaluation metrics :

A vital part of evaluating a model is using metrics to measure its performance. These metrics enable us to quantify a model's effectiveness in specific tasks, and to compare it with other models.

Precision is a common metric that indicates the percentage of correct predictions made by the model. Recall, on the other hand, measures the proportion of actual positive results that the model has correctly identified. AUC-ROC (Area Under the Receiver Operating Characteristic Curve) is another popular metric used in model evaluation. It evaluates a model's performance at different classification thresholds and is particularly useful for binary classification tasks.

AI evaluation metrics, such as precision, recall and AUC-ROC, are essential for quantifying the performance of a machine learning model. Each metric brings its own perspective on model performance and, by using them together, we can get a complete picture of model quality.

To illustrate, let's consider a machine learning model designed to predict whether an email is spam or not. In this context, "accuracy" refers to the percentage of emails that the model has correctly identified as spam out of all the emails it has identified as such. So, if the model predicts 100 emails as spam and 90 of them are actually spam, then the accuracy is 90%.

Recall", on the other hand, focuses on how many emails are actually spam and how many the model has managed to identify correctly. So, if out of 100 emails that are really spam, the model correctly identifies 80, the recall is 80%.

Both metrics are important, but they don't give the full picture. For example, a model may have 100% accuracy by marking only one email as spam and making sure it is, but this doesn't mean it's good at catching all spam emails, it has simply avoided making mistakes in its predictions.

This is where AUC-ROC comes in. This metric compares the rate of true positives (emails that are actually spam and that the model has correctly identified as such) with the rate of false positives (emails that are not spam, but that the model has identified as such). AUC-ROC gives an indication of the model's overall performance at different classification thresholds. An AUC-ROC value of 1.0 means that the model distinguished perfectly between spam and non-spam emails at all thresholds, while a value of 0.5 means that it did no better than a random draw.

By taking these three metrics into account, we can get a complete picture of a model's performance. Precision gives us an idea of the reliability of the model's predictions, recall tells us how many positive results the model is capable of capturing, and AUC-ROC gives us an assessment of the model's overall performance across different thresholds. It's therefore important to use a set of these metrics to assess the quality and efficiency of a machine learning model.

Each of these metrics offers a different perspective on a model's performance, and it's important to take them into account to get a complete view of model efficiency.

Overlearning and underlearning

Overlearning and underlearning are two major obstacles that can hamper the accuracy and efficiency of machine learning models. These problems are particularly noticeable when models are put to the test with new or unpublished data.

Take, for example, a machine learning model designed to distinguish photos of cats from those of dogs. If overlearned, the model could become too specialized in recognizing the photos in the training set. If, for example, all the cats in the learning set are Siamese, the model may learn to recognize this breed specifically, but fail to recognize other cat breeds correctly. It's like a student memorizing the questions and answers of a specific exam, without understanding the underlying concepts - he might do well if the next exam had exactly the same questions, but fail if he had to apply his knowledge to different questions.

Underlearning, on the other hand, occurs when the model is not sufficiently complex or detailed to capture all the important aspects of the data. Let's return to our example of classifying photos of dogs and cats. Suppose our model is too simple and relies solely on color to make the distinction. If a dog is gray, like most of the cats in the learning set, the model could misclassify it as a cat. This is comparable to a student who studies only part of the course material before an exam - he may answer some questions correctly, but is likely to fail those on topics he hasn't studied.

Navigating between overlearning and underlearning is a tricky aspect of training machine learning models. It's all about striking the right balance between a model that learns enough from the training data to make good predictions, without becoming distracted by noise or irrelevant details. Techniques such as cross-validation, regularization and model parameter tuning can help achieve this balance. Avoiding bias and variance requires a delicate balance, and is an essential aspect of model optimization.

Optimizing hyperparameters :

Optimizing hyperparameters is another major step in the process of creating machine learning models. Hyperparameters are model parameters that are defined prior to training and are not learned from the data. These parameters can have a significant impact on model performance.

There are several techniques for optimizing hyperparameters. Grid search is a method used to optimize the hyperparameters of a machine learning model. The idea is to define a grid of hyperparameters to be tested and systematically try out all possible combinations to identify the one that gives the best results.

Let's take the example of a Random Forest model, which is a type of machine learning algorithm based on decision trees. Key hyperparameters for a random forest include the number of trees (n_estimators) and the maximum depth of each tree (max_depth). To optimize these hyperparameters, we could define a grid of possible values for each: for example, n_estimators could vary from 10 to 100 in increments of 10, and max_depth could vary from 1 to 10.

In this case, the grid search will systematically test all combinations of n_estimators and max_depth within these ranges. It will start, for example, with n_estimators=10 and max_depth=1, then n_estimators=10 and max_depth=2, and so on, until n_estimators=100 and max_depth=10. For each combination, it will train a random forest model, evaluate it (using cross-validation, for example), and retain the model's performance.

Once all combinations have been tested, the grid search selects the hyperparameter values that gave the best performance and uses these values to build the final model. In our example, it might turn out that n_estimators=70 and max_depth=5 give the best balance between bias and variance, producing the best performing model on the test data.

It's important to note that grid search can be very costly in terms of time and resources, as it requires the training and evaluation of numerous models. Furthermore, it doesn't necessarily guarantee finding the global optimum, especially if the optimal values lie outside the range defined for the grid. Despite these challenges, grid search remains a commonly used technique for hyperparameter optimization, due to its simplicity and ability to systematically explore the parameter space.

Random search is a hyperparameter optimization method that involves randomly selecting combinations of hyperparameters to train a machine learning model. In contrast to grid search, which systematically explores all possible hyperparameter combinations, random search can explore the hyperparameter space in a much more flexible and potentially more efficient way.

To illustrate how random search works, imagine you're training a random forest model, which has several key hyperparameters such as the number of trees in the forest (n_estimators), the maximum tree depth (max_depth), and the minimum number of samples required to split an internal node (min_samples_split). Instead of specifying specific values for these hyperparameters, you specify ranges of possible values. For example, you could say that n_estimators could be any integer between 50 and 200, max_depth could be any integer between 10 and 20, and min_samples_split could be any integer between 2 and 5.

Then, for each iteration of training, Random Search chooses a random number of estimators, a maximum depth, and a minimum number of samples to divide a node from the ranges you've specified, then trains the model with these hyperparameters. It repeats this process for a number of iterations, each time recording the model's performance on a validation set. At the end, it selects the combination of hyperparameters that gave the best performance on the validation set.

Random search can be particularly effective when you have a large number of hyperparameters and you don't know which are the most important. In these cases, random search can sometimes find better hyperparameter combinations in less time than grid search, because it can explore more hyperparameter space with the same number of iterations. For example, if you have 10 hyperparameters and you try 100 combinations, grid search will only let you explore 10 combinations per hyperparameter, whereas random search will let you explore 100 different combinations for each hyperparameter.

More recently, reinforcement learning is an approach to artificial intelligence inspired by the way living beings learn by trial and error. The idea is to train an agent to make decisions by offering it a reward or punishment based on the results of its actions. The agent then learns to maximize long-term rewards by adopting an optimal action strategy.

In the context of hyperparameter optimization, one could conceive of reinforcement learning as a process in which an agent (the hyperparameter optimization algorithm) explores the space of hyperparameters and receives a reward based on the model's performance with the chosen hyperparameters. For example, in the case of a neural network, hyperparameters could include the size of the network (the number of layers and neurons per layer), the learning rate, the type of activation function, and so on.

The agent could start by randomly selecting values for these hyperparameters, then evaluate the model's performance (for example, its error rate on a validation set). The model's performance is then used as a reward signal for the agent. If the model performs well, the agent receives a high reward and is therefore encouraged to choose similar hyperparameter values in the future. If the model performs badly, the agent receives a small reward (or punishment), and learns to avoid these hyperparameter values.

Over time, by exploring and exploiting the space of hyperparameters, the agent learns a strategy for choosing the hyperparameters that maximize model performance. In other words, it learns to optimize hyperparameters.

A concrete example of this concept is Google DeepMind's work on hyperparameter optimization using reinforcement learning. They trained a reinforcement learning agent to optimize the hyperparameters of a neural network for an image classification task. The agent was able to learn a hyperparameter optimization strategy that outperformed traditional optimization methods, demonstrating the potential of reinforcement learning for hyperparameter optimization.

Arguably, model evaluation and optimization are indispensable aspects of the machine learning process. They enable us to ensure that the models we create are not only efficient, but also robust, reliable and suited to the task for which they are intended.

How conversational models work

The Transformer model :

Conversational models like GPT, which is based on the Transformer architecture, use a natural language processing approach known as "deep learning". Transformer models can be quite complex to operate, but at the heart of this complexity is a series of mathematical calculations applied to numerical representations of words, called embeddings.

Let's start with a basic example. Let's imagine we ask the model to complete the sentence "The cat is on the...". The model receives this input as a sequence of words and transforms it into a series of numerical vectors, one for each word. These vectors, which are the embeddings, capture the semantic information of the words in the sentence.

Next, the Transformer model applies a series of mathematical transformations to these vectors. It starts with multi-head attention, which allows the model to focus its "attention" on different parts of the sentence when generating an answer. For our example, this means that when the model generates the next word after "the cat is on the...", it can take into account both "the cat" and "is on the" to decide which word is more likely.

Next, the model adds these transformed vectors to their originals (known as "residuals") and applies layer normalization to help stabilize the learning process. These vectors are then passed through another series of transformations, including a fully connected layer, before ending up in the same form as at the start - a series of vectors, one for each word position.

Finally, the model applies a softmax function to the scores of each possible word in the vocabulary, resulting in a probability distribution over the words. The word with the highest probability is chosen as the next word in the sequence. In our example, the most likely word after "The cat is on the..." could be "roof", so the model would generate this response.

This process occurs at each time step, enabling the model to generate responses word by word. It's important to note that, although each word is generated individually, the model takes the whole sentence into account thanks to multi-headed attention. This means that although the model generates a word-by-word response, each word is informed by the context of the whole sentence.

Beyond this basic process, there are many details and nuances to the exact workings of Transformer models, including how they are trained on large amounts of text and how they can be fine-tuned for specific tasks. However, the essential point is that these models use a series of mathematical transformations to convert sentences into numerical representations, and then use these representations to generate responses based on context and probability.

The Transformer is based primarily on a notion called "attention", which in this context refers to a model's ability to focus on certain parts of an input when generating an output. For example, if you have the sentence "Cats like to chase mice", when generating the word "chase", the model "pays attention" mainly to the word "cats". This is a major advance on previous models, such as Recurrent Neural Networks (RNN), which processed information sequentially, making them less effective at capturing long-term dependencies in text.

The evolution of Transformers: from GPT-1 to GPT-4 by OpenAI

Since the development of Transformers technology in 2017, the field of artificial intelligence has seen significant advances. OpenAI, an organization at the forefront of AI, has been particularly successful in leveraging the core principles of Transformers to create a series of highly innovative language models called Generative Pretrained Transformers, or GPTs. From GPT-1 to GPT-3, the impact of these models on machine understanding of natural language has been profound.

GPT-1: The first steps towards generative AI

The first in this series, GPT-1, was unveiled in 2018. With its 117 million parameters, this model laid the foundations for future innovations by demonstrating the possibility of generating coherent and often relevant text from raw web data. GPT-1 used unsupervised learning to understand and reproduce complex linguistic patterns, marking a milestone in the development of generative language models.

GPT-2: Awe and controversy

The release of GPT-2 in 2019 has taken this technology one step further. With its 1.5 billion parameters, GPT-2 showed a significant improvement in the ability to generate realistic text. This has sparked controversy as much as wonder. Fearing malicious use of its technology, OpenAI initially chose not to publish the full model. This event launched a wider debate on the ethical and safety implications of generative AI.

GPT-3: towards advanced language understanding

In 2020, GPT-3 arrived, pushing the boundaries even further. This model, composed of a mind-boggling 175 billion parameters, took text generation to the next level. GPT-3's ability to understand language and generate text was so advanced that users began using it for a wide range of applications, from writing e-mails to creating poems, and much more.

GPT-4: a new step towards artificial intelligence

While the Transformers story is still being written, an exciting new chapter is taking shape with the arrival of GPT-4. Although GPT-4 is still in development at my last point of knowledge in September 2021, we can speculate based on previous evolutions of this model series what GPT-4 might offer.

With each new release of GPT, OpenAI has systematically pushed back the boundaries of what language models can achieve. It's reasonable to assume that GPT-4 will continue on this path, offering a substantial improvement in text generation and language understanding over GPT-3.

GPT-4 could potentially have trillions of parameters, enabling even more advanced language understanding and text generation. We could expect improvements in the model's ability to understand context, capture subtle nuances and generate even more precise and appropriate responses.

This could enable more sophisticated applications, from the generation of even more creative and original content, to AI-based decision support, to even more natural interactions with users. GPT-4 could also help advance areas such as machine translation, sentiment analysis and much more.

In terms of learning and optimization, GPT-4 could benefit from advances in training techniques, such as federated learning methods or new forms of regularization. This could lead to improved training efficiency and better generalization from training data.

It's also likely that GPT-4 will emphasize transparency and interpretability, in response to concerns about AI's "black boxes". This means that GPT-4 could be designed to explain its own thought processes, making its decisions and responses more understandable to users.

However, like its predecessors, GPT-4 will also bring its own ethical and safety challenges. More powerful models are also more likely to be abused, requiring appropriate regulation and robust security measures.

Overall, as we eagerly await the release of GPT-4, it's clear that each new model in OpenAI's GPT series is not just a technological breakthrough, but also an opportunity to reflect on how we integrate and manage AI in our society.

Beyond GPT-4 :

The advances made by GPT-1, GPT-2, GPT-3 and GPT-4 in the field of artificial intelligence have opened up new possibilities for natural language processing. However, as these technologies become increasingly sophisticated, it is imperative that we continue to evaluate and address the ethical implications of their use. As we look to the future, OpenAI's GPT model series offers us a glimpse of the immense potential (and challenges) that generative AI can bring to society.

The next generation of GPT models and other Transformer-based technologies promise to continue improving our interaction with machines. The future of AI is incredibly bright, and OpenAI's work gives us a glimpse of what lies ahead.

How ChatGPT uses the Transformer model

ChatGPT is a variant of these GPT templates, specially trained to generate conversational chat responses. To understand how this works, we first need to understand that GPT templates are trained in two stages: pre-training and fine-training.

During pre-training, the model learns to predict the next word in a sentence based on a large number of texts on the web. This enables it to learn general knowledge about the world, as well as the grammar and vocabulary of the language. Then, during fine-training, the model is trained on a specific dataset so that it can perform the desired task. For ChatGPT, this task is to generate chat responses. The fine-training dataset includes conversations where humans played both roles: that of the user and that of the AI assistant.

The combination of pre-training and fine-tuning enables ChatGPT to interact with users in a compelling and useful way, while harnessing the power of the Transformer architecture to understand and generate text.

Transform and GPT are the key elements that make ChatGPT and other advanced language models possible. By understanding these technologies, we can better grasp the capabilities and limitations of the AI tools we use today, as well as the opportunities they could offer in the future.

The learning process

Artificial intelligence, particularly language models like ChatGPT, learns through a process known as machine learning. In simple terms, machine learning enables systems to learn automatically from experience without being explicitly programmed. They do this by using algorithms which, through iterative methods, improve their performance by feeding on more and more data.

For example, imagine a child learning to recognize animals. As he is shown different pictures of dogs and told that each picture represents a dog, the child begins to understand what a dog is and to distinguish it from other animals. In the same way, a language model is formed by showing him many sentences and teaching him to predict the words that follow in these sentences.

Supervised learning: how ChatGPT is trained

ChatGPT, like most language models, is trained using a method known as supervised learning. Supervised learning is achieved by presenting the AI with examples of input and output data. For example, ChatGPT can be given a sentence and asked to predict the next word in the sentence. As the model sees more and more examples, it adjusts the weights of its neurons to minimize the error between its predictions and the true answers. Let's imagine that ChatGPT is given the beginning of a sentence like "The sky is...". In the training data, there will probably be many examples where this sentence is followed by the word "blue". Through supervised learning, ChatGPT learns that the word "blue" is a plausible response after "The sky is...". Of course, the process is far more complex and takes thousands of factors into account, but that's the basic idea.

The role of training data in ChatGPT training

Training data is essential to the training of any language model, including ChatGPT. This data is typically a large set of texts from a variety of sources, such as books, newspaper articles and websites. Models learn by assimilating the linguistic patterns and structures present in this data. By analyzing this data, ChatGPT learns not only the grammar and vocabulary of the language, but also facts about the world, common opinions, and even certain biases present in the texts. It's important to note that the quality of the responses generated by ChatGPT is highly dependent on the quality of the training data. If the data is of poor quality, poorly written or biased, the model will generate lower-quality responses.

Learning transfer and the importance of Fine-Tuning

Once a language model like ChatGPT has been pre-trained on a large dataset, it can be adapted to specific tasks through a process called "fine-tuning" or "transfer learning". This involves taking the pre-trained model and further training it on a smaller, task-specific dataset. Suppose we want ChatGPT to answer medical questions. After initial training, the model has a basic understanding of the language and a general knowledge of the world. However, it doesn't necessarily understand medical terminology or concepts specific to medicine. To specialize it, we could fine-tune it using a dataset of medical questions and answers. In this way, the model can transfer what it has learned during initial training and apply it to this new task.

The process of learning the language model is a complex and sophisticated one, involving supervised learning, training data and learning transfer. Together, these components enable ChatGPT to understand and generate language in impressive ways, paving the way for exciting and innovative applications.

Text generation

Text generation, the fundamental technology that powers language models such as ChatGPT, has transformed the way we interact with machines, ushering in a new era in artificial intelligence. This technology goes far beyond traditional approaches to human-machine dialogue, which were based on predefined responses or conditioned by strict rules. Today, thanks to the evolution of AI, we are able to conduct dynamic, nuanced conversations with machines, exchanges that seem incredibly human in their fluidity and adaptability. To fully appreciate the scope of this revolution, it is essential to understand two key concepts underlying this technology: natural language processing (NLP) and text generation.

Natural language processing is a field of artificial intelligence that focuses on the interaction between computers and human language. It encompasses a variety of tasks, from speech recognition to automatic question answering and sentiment analysis. NLP is basically an attempt to translate our complex and often ambiguous natural language into something a machine can understand, process and use.

Text generation is a sub-discipline of NLP that focuses specifically on a computer's ability to produce text that is comprehensible, coherent and contextually relevant to humans. This is where the real magic of models like ChatGPT lies. Whereas in the past, text generation was based on rule models or predefined responses, today, thanks to advances such as Transformer-based language models, we have systems that can produce text that not only sounds human, but is also adaptive, reflecting the nuances of the input prompt and generating responses that are contextually appropriate.

These advances have paved the way for an incredibly wide range of applications, from automatic content creation to customer support, education and more. Yet, despite the progress made, it's important to note that text generation is an area of active research, with many challenges ahead, such as improving the accuracy, interpretability and ethics of models. By exploring these key concepts and understanding the basic principles, we can better appreciate the scope of this technology and its potential impact on our digital future.

Natural language understanding and text generation

Natural language understanding is a sub-discipline of artificial intelligence that focuses on the interaction between computers and human language. It enables machines to read, understand and derive meaning from human language in a valuable way. For example, when you ask your voice assistant to read the latest news, it's NLP that enables it to understand your request and respond accordingly.

Text generation, on the other hand, is the process by which artificial intelligence produces human-readable text. It relies on NLP to create responses or narratives that go beyond simple predetermined answers. For example, if you ask your AI assistant to tell you a story, text generation enables the AI to create a coherent, captivating story from scratch.

How ChatGPT generates responses from prompts

ChatGPT, a language model developed by OpenAI, uses natural language understanding and text generation to produce dynamic responses to prompts. Based on the Transformer architecture, it is trained on a vast corpus of Internet text to learn linguistic patterns and language structure.

When a prompt is provided, ChatGPT uses what it has learned to generate an appropriate response. If you give this language model the prompt "What is photosynthesis?", it will generate a detailed response explaining the process by which plants use sunlight to convert carbon dioxide and water into glucose and oxygen.

What's really impressive is that ChatGPT doesn't just look for a predefined answer in a database. Instead, it "improvises" its answer based on what it has learned in training. It draws on its knowledge to formulate a coherent, relevant response to the question posed.

Dialogue management and real-time interaction

Another important feature of ChatGPT is its ability to handle dynamic dialogues and real-time interactions. Unlike some older AI systems that can only handle simple queries, ChatGPT can participate in more complex conversations.

For example, if you ask ChatGPT to help you write a cover letter for a software engineering position, it may ask you questions to gather more information, such as relevant past experience or specific skills. It then uses this information to generate a personalized cover letter that highlights your qualifications for the position.

Ultimately, what makes this language model so powerful is its ability to understand and generate text flexibly and dynamically. It can participate in complex conversations, react to topic changes and generate creative responses, making it an extremely useful tool for a variety of applications, from article writing to homework assistance to creative writing coaching. It's a truly game-changing technology, pushing back the boundaries of what AI can achieve, and paving the way for a future where machines will be able to understand and interact with human language in increasingly sophisticated ways.

Limitations and challenges

Artificial intelligence, although it has transformed various aspects of our lives, still has significant limitations that deserve our attention. One of the major criticisms of AI concerns the "black box" problem, a metaphor that illustrates how these systems, particularly deep neural networks, make decisions.

Imagine a sophisticated coffee machine: you insert a capsule, press a button and get a cup of coffee. You know the machine works, but the exact process of transforming the capsule into coffee remains obscure. Similarly, advanced AI models like ChatGPT ingest immense amounts of data (the capsules), apply complex algorithms (the internal machinery) and produce predictions or decisions (the coffee), but the exact process of how they arrive at these conclusions often remains opaque.

This opacity can cause problems, particularly when it comes to critical decision-making. If an AI system is used to evaluate loan applications and rejects an application, it is essential for the borrower to understand why their application was rejected. However, with today's artificial intelligence, providing a clear explanation that humans can understand is a challenge.

Ethical and bias challenges in artificial intelligence

Ethics and bias are two other major problems associated with AI. Machine learning models, such as ChatGPT, are trained on huge amounts of text data from the web. Unfortunately, this data can reflect and perpetuate existing biases in society.

For example, if an AI model is trained on data that includes a gender bias, it could end up reproducing this bias in its responses. If we use such a model for recruitment, for example, it could unconsciously favor one gender over another, which can lead to discrimination.

Ethical challenges also arise in contexts where AI is used to make decisions that have real consequences for people's lives. For example, AI is increasingly used in healthcare to help diagnose and treat patients. However, it is essential to ensure that AI is used ethically and responsibly in these contexts, respecting the confidentiality and security of patient data, while providing high-quality care.

The next steps: towards more transparent and equitable AI

Faced with these challenges, researchers are actively working to develop more transparent and fair artificial intelligence methods. When it comes to transparency, there is a growing interest in explainable artificial intelligence, which aims to make intelligent machine processes more understandable to humans. Rather than simply providing a prediction or decision, an explainable AI model could also provide an explanation of how it arrived at that prediction or decision.

With regard to fairness, efforts are being made to develop methods for detecting and mitigating bias in conversational models. Tools are being developed to analyze the output of AI models for signs of bias. In addition, "fair re-learning" techniques are being explored to adjust conversational models to reduce bias.

However, these efforts are still ongoing, and much work remains to be done. As we continue to integrate artificial intelligence into our lives, it's essential to keep these limitations and challenges in mind, and to work actively to create AI that is not only powerful and efficient, but also transparent, fair and ethical.

-3-

The impact of AI on everyday life

"Artificial intelligence is a tool, not a threat."

Rodney Brooks

Reimagining life and work in the age of AI

A new engine for social transformation

Artificial intelligence is not just an innovative technology, it's a powerful engine of social transformation that's changing the way we live, work and interact with the world around us. By modifying traditional sectors, creating new industries and reshaping our daily lives, artificial intelligence is actively shaping our future.

AI's impact on traditional industries

Traditional industries, whether manufacturing, healthcare or retail, are not immune to the changes brought about by AI.

Take manufacturing, for example. In the past, production processes were generally manual and laborious. However, with the introduction of artificial intelligence, we have seen a significant increase in automation. AI-powered robots can now perform repetitive tasks faster and with greater precision than humans. Tesla, for example, has integrated intelligent robots into its production lines, improving efficiency and quality while reducing costs.

In the healthcare field, AI has enabled major advances, such as computer-aided diagnosis. Machine learning algorithms are now able to analyze medical images to detect abnormalities such as tumors, often with equal or greater accuracy than doctors. For example, Google Health has developed an AI system that can detect breast cancer on mammograms with an accuracy comparable to that of human radiologists.

The emergence of new business sectors thanks to AI

Alongside the transformation of traditional industries, artificial intelligence has given rise to entirely new business sectors. One of the most striking examples is the autonomous vehicle sector. AI, combined with other technologies such as sensors and GPS, has made it possible to design vehicles that can travel safely without a human driver. Companies like Waymo, a subsidiary of Alphabet Inc. are actively working on commercializing this technology, paving the way for a future where autonomous cars could become the norm.

Similarly, AI has paved the way for the emergence of the virtual assistant sector. Devices such as Amazon Echo, Google Home or Apple Siri, use artificial intelligence to understand and respond to users' vocal requests, creating a totally new and intuitive user interface.

AI in everyday life:

Outside the world of work, artificial intelligence has also begun to infiltrate our daily lives in significant ways. Whether through personalized recommendations on Netflix or Spotify, real-time traffic prediction on Google Maps, or helping us manage our finances via fintech apps, AI is increasingly ubiquitous.

What's more, artificial intelligence has significant potential to make our daily lives easier. For example, AI is being used in smart homes to automate a variety of tasks, from adjusting lighting and temperature based on occupant preferences, to predicting grocery needs based on eating habits.

In short, AI is transforming our society at a rapid pace. By modifying traditional industries, creating new ones, and transforming our daily lives, artificial intelligence is truly a powerful driver of societal transformation. We therefore need to understand these changes and adapt our skills and attitudes to succeed in the AI era.

The challenges and opportunities of AI

How AI is redefining the world of work

With the rise of Artificial Intelligence, the world of work is rapidly transforming. Many industries have already begun to integrate the intelligent machine into their operations, leading to significant changes in the way work is done.

Take the automotive industry, for example. Historically, car production was a laborious process requiring many human workers. Today, many factory tasks are automated thanks to the intelligent machine. Robots guided by artificial intelligence assemble vehicles with unrivalled precision and speed, reducing errors and boosting productivity.

But it's not just in manufacturing that artificial intelligence is making its presence felt. In the healthcare sector, AI is being used to analyze medical records, aid diagnosis and even predict the likelihood of certain diseases based on patient data. In the financial sector, automated trading algorithms process billions of transactions every day, and AI-based chatbots provide 24/7 customer services.

AI and the skills of the future

With AI taking over more and more tasks, the skills required in the workplace are also changing. Technical skills related to artificial intelligence, such as machine learning and data analysis, are increasingly in demand. But it's not just technical skills that are important. While AI is excellent at handling routine, data-driven tasks, it cannot yet replicate unique human skills, such as creativity, critical thinking and emotional intelligence. These "soft" skills are becoming increasingly valuable as AI transforms the workplace.

For example, while an algorithm can analyze data on consumer behavior, it's still up to a human to understand the context of that data, devise a creative marketing strategy, or navigate complex customer interactions.

The challenges of AI: automation and job transformation

While artificial intelligence offers many opportunities, it also presents significant challenges. The most obvious is the impact on employment. According to a McKinsey report, up to 30% of today's tasks could be automated by 2030 as a result of artificial intelligence. This could lead to major disruption in the labor market, with jobs lost in some sectors and new jobs created in others.

For example, truck drivers could see their jobs threatened by the advent of autonomous vehicles. However, demand for AI professionals, data managers and other technology-related roles is likely to increase.

It's also important to note that AI can increase inequality if its benefits are not distributed fairly. People with advanced technical skills are likely to be able to benefit from AI, while those with less specialized skills could find themselves at a disadvantage.

In short, while the intelligent machine redefines the world of work and demands new skills, it also presents significant challenges in terms of automation and job transformation. It is essential to understand these challenges and seek solutions to ensure a fair transition to an increasingly automated economy.

AI and society: ethical and moral implications

As Artificial Intelligence develops and becomes more pervasive in our lives, questions of ethics and morality take on paramount importance. It is essential to address these issues to ensure responsible and beneficial use of this technology for all. In this chapter, we will explore three main aspects of this issue: the transparency and fairness of artificial intelligence, privacy and security issues, and the regulatory challenges associated with artificial intelligence.

AI transparency and fairness

Transparency refers to the ability to understand how a machine works and makes decisions. For example, if an AI model is used to evaluate loan applications, it is necessary to understand how it calculates credit risk. This ensures not only that the model is efficient and correct, but also that it doesn't discriminate against certain groups of people on the basis of factors such as race, gender, age, etc.

Fairness, on the other hand, is a question of social justice. AI models should be designed to be fair and non-discriminatory. The AI system used for facial recognition should not be less accurate for people of color, or for women versus men. To achieve this goal, it is important to ensure that the data used to train these models is representative of all the populations concerned.

Privacy and security issues in AI

Privacy and security are two other major AI issues. For example, if you use a voice assistant such as ChatGPT, you would want to be sure that your conversations are not being recorded or used for unwanted purposes. In addition, it's important that these systems are secure against malicious attacks that might seek to exploit their capabilities for harmful activities.

Confidentiality is particularly delicate when artificial intelligence is used in sensitive contexts such as healthcare or finance. An AI system used to analyze medical data must be designed to protect patient confidentiality. Engineers need to work closely with legislators and ethicists to ensure that such systems meet the highest standards of confidentiality and security.

AI and Governance: Regulatory Challenges

Finally, AI poses numerous regulatory challenges. How can we regulate a technology that is evolving faster than our ability to understand it and frame it legally? How can we ensure that companies developing and using AI do so ethically and responsibly? And how can we ensure that the benefits of artificial intelligence are shared equitably, without exacerbating existing inequalities?

An example of this challenge is the current debate surrounding facial recognition. Some argue for a total ban on this technology because of its potential violations of privacy, while others support its regulated use for specific use cases, such as crime-fighting. It's important to strike a balance between technological innovation and the protection of human rights.

All in all, these issues highlight the importance of a thoughtful and ethical approach to AI. As we continue to explore and harness the potential of this technology, we need to engage in an open and constructive dialogue on these issues to ensure that the intelligent machine is used in a way that benefits everyone and respects our core values.

AI and education: preparing the next generation

In the context of the rapid acceleration of artificial intelligence technologies, the field of education is set to play a leading role. At the intersection of technological innovation and the training of tomorrow's citizens, we explore in this chapter how artificial intelligence can transform the education sector, the challenges to be met and the ways in which education can be adapted to prepare future generations for the age of the intelligent machine. In addition, we analyze the role of continuing education in a society where artificial intelligence is becoming increasingly important.

AI in Education:

AI offers fascinating possibilities for education. Adaptive teaching systems, powered by AI, can offer personalized learning for every student. These systems can track an individual's learning pace, identify their strengths and weaknesses, and adapt content accordingly. A case in point is the "Knewton" platform, which offers adaptive learning in math and English.

AI can also facilitate access to education. Educational chatbots, for example, can help students at any time, reducing geographical and temporal barriers to learning. Duolingo, a language learning platform, uses AI to personalize lessons and offers a chatbot for conversational practice.

However, the integration of artificial intelligence into education also raises challenges. Concerns about equity and fairness arise when not everyone has access to the same technological resources. Moreover, over-reliance on artificial intelligence could lead to a dehumanization of education. Finally, protecting students' privacy is a major issue, as AI systems need large amounts of data to operate effectively.

Training future generations in AI

In the age of the intelligent machine, education must evolve to prepare students for a world where interaction with AI will be commonplace. This involves not only teaching technical skills, such as programming and understanding the principles of artificial intelligence, but also teaching critical thinking about artificial intelligence. Students must learn to ask ethical questions about the use of the intelligent machine, understand possible biases in AI systems and think about the societal implications of artificial intelligence.

For example, the Montfort high school in France has launched a program that includes robotics and programming from an early age. In high school, students take a course on the ethics of artificial intelligence. This holistic approach ensures that students are not just passive consumers of technology, but active, informed citizens in the age of AI.

The role of continuing education

As AI transforms the world of work, continuing education plays an increasingly important role. It's no longer enough to learn a skill and practice it for an entire career. Instead, workers must constantly update their skills to stay relevant.

Online platforms such as Coursera and Udacity offer courses in artificial intelligence and machine learning. These platforms enable individuals from all professions to acquire relevant AI skills, often with the guidance of expert instructors and hands-on project opportunities. However, continuing education is not limited to technical learning. As AI takes over more and more routine tasks, human skills such as creativity, empathy and ethical judgment become increasingly important. Continuing education programs must therefore adopt a balanced approach, emphasizing both technical and human skills.

AI is having a profound impact on education, offering exciting opportunities, but also significant challenges. To effectively prepare future generations for the age of the intelligent machine, we need to rethink our approach to education, focusing on comprehensive training and lifelong continuing education.

AI evolution gas pedals:

The digital transformation we are currently experiencing is marked by an exponential growth in the amount of data produced every day. From exchanging messages on social networks to Internet of Things sensors, from reading online content to commercial transactions, data generation is omnipresent. In this context, artificial intelligence, in particular machine learning, plays a major role, transforming this data into useful, actionable knowledge. However, the abundance of data also presents significant challenges in terms of management and processing.

The exponential growth of data

We live in an era where data is being generated at a rate never seen before. According to an IDC report, around 59 zettabytes of data were created or copied worldwide in 2020, and this number is expected to reach 175 zettabytes by 2025. This is such an immense volume of data that it's hard to visualize: one zettabyte is equivalent to one trillion gigabytes!

This data explosion is fuelled by a number of factors. The increasing digitization of our lives, the rise of social media, the development of the Internet of Things, and the expansion of e-commerce are just some of the drivers of this growth. For example, every minute, nearly 500 hours of video are uploaded to YouTube, over 4.1 million videos are viewed, and over 2.2 million pieces of content are shared on Facebook.

The importance of data for machine learning

In this context, AI, and more specifically machine learning, is the tool par excellence for transforming this raw data into meaningful information. This is because machine learning models learn from data: the more and the more diverse the data, the more the models can improve and refine their predictions.

For example, consider a machine learning model designed to recognize images of cats. To do this, it needs lots of cat photos to learn to recognize the various features that define a cat: eye shape, ear size, coat texture, etc. If you provide it with millions of cat images of all kinds, the model will be able to recognize a cat with great accuracy, whatever the breed, posture or color of the cat.

The challenges of processing massive data

However, the abundance of data also poses major challenges. The first is the challenge of storage: where to store all this data in a secure and accessible way? Solutions such as cloud storage offer an answer, but they also raise questions of security and confidentiality.

The second challenge is analysis. How do you extract useful information from this ocean of data? This is where machine learning algorithms come in, but training these models on large datasets can be costly in terms of time and computing resources.

The third challenge is data quality. Not all data is useful or relevant, and some may even be misleading or biased. Data preparation, involving the cleaning and selection of appropriate data for machine learning, is an important but laborious step in the process. The explosion of data presents both opportunities and challenges for AI. On the one hand, it provides the "fuel" that machine learning models need to learn and improve. On the other, it poses data management, analysis and quality issues that need to be carefully managed to make the most of this wealth of information. As we move further into the digital age, the ability to navigate this ever-changing data landscape will become increasingly important.

Technological advances: from hardware to algorithms

Technological advances in the field of artificial intelligence are impressive and occurring at a breathtaking pace. These advances range from cutting-edge hardware to sophisticated machine learning algorithms, creating a constantly evolving technological landscape. To understand how these advances are contributing to the rapid evolution of AI, it is essential to examine developments in computing hardware, machine learning algorithms, and the synergistic interactions between hardware and software.

Advances in computing hardware

Advances in computing hardware have been one of the driving forces behind the rise of AI. Graphics processing units (GPUs), in particular, have played a major role in this evolution. Originally designed to accelerate graphics operations in video games, GPUs have found a new use in parallel computing, an essential feature for processing the large volumes of data used in machine learning.

To illustrate this evolution, let's take the example of Nvidia, a major player in the GPU field. In 2020, Nvidia launched the Ampere A100, a massively parallel GPU offering 312 teraflops of performance for mixed precision operations, making it ideal for machine learning and deep learning. These computing capabilities have enabled significant advances in the training of deep neural networks, making it possible to process huge datasets and improve the performance of AI models.

Innovations in machine learning algorithms

Alongside advances in hardware, innovations in machine learning algorithms have been equally important to the progress of AI. These algorithms, which are the mechanisms by which machines learn from data, have become increasingly sophisticated and efficient.

A concrete example of this innovation is the rise of convolutional neural networks (CNNs), which have revolutionized the field of computer vision. CNNs use a specific structure of layers of neurons to filter and process images hierarchically, enabling them to accurately recognize shapes, textures and objects in images.

Another major example is the emergence of transformers, a type of language model that has enabled significant advances in natural language processing (NLP). The transformer, first introduced in the "Attention is All You Need" paper in 2017, has since been the foundation of many powerful language models, including GPT-3.

Synergistic interactions between hardware and software in AI

Technological advances in AI are not simply the sum of independent developments in hardware and algorithms. There is a synergistic interaction between hardware and software, where advances in one feed into and stimulate progress in the other.

For example, GPU improvements have enabled the creation and training of deeper and more complex neural networks, which in turn has stimulated hardware innovation to meet the growing demand for computing power. Similarly, advances in machine learning algorithms, such as efficient learning methods and optimized network architectures, have led to more efficient use of existing hardware, enabling AI models to run on a wider range of devices, including smartphones and microcontrollers. Technological advances in computational hardware and machine learning algorithms, and the synergistic interactions between them, have been key to the rapid rise of AI. Understanding these developments helps us to grasp not only where we are now, but also to glimpse the future possibilities of AI.

The growing adoption of AI by companies and institutions

As artificial intelligence continues to evolve, companies and institutions around the world are looking to adopt these technologies to improve their operations, better serve their customers and remain competitive in an increasingly digitized world. This growing adoption of AI has profound implications for how we do business, how we govern and how we live.

AI as a competitive advantage

For businesses, AI offers an incredible competitive advantage. It can analyze large amounts of data at unprecedented speed and accuracy, providing valuable insights into customers, the market and internal operations.

For example, imagine a retail company using AI to analyze its customers' buying habits. AI can identify trends, predict future behavior and offer personalized product recommendations. This enables the company to increase sales, improve customer satisfaction and build customer loyalty.

AI can also be used to automate routine and time-consuming tasks, enabling employees to focus on more complex and creative tasks. A logistics company could, for example, use AI to automate inventory tracking and route planning, improving efficiency and reducing costs.

Case studies: companies leading the AI revolution

Many companies are at the forefront of the AI revolution. Take Google, for example, which has embraced AI at every level of its organization. They use AI to improve their search services, develop cutting-edge machine learning technologies and even optimize the energy efficiency of their data centers.

Another example is Netflix, which uses AI to recommend movies and TV series to its users. By analyzing its users' viewing habits, preferences and behaviors, Netflix can offer personalized recommendations, enhancing the user experience and encouraging users to spend more time on the platform. They are far from alone. Many other companies have embraced AI, paving the way for unprecedented innovation.

Amazon is one of the leaders in AI. The e-commerce giant uses AI for everything from demand prediction to product recommendation. Amazon has also pioneered virtual assistants with Alexa, which uses natural language processing algorithms to understand and respond to users' voice queries. In addition, Amazon Web Services offers a range of AI-based services, enabling companies in all sectors to easily integrate AI into their operations.

Tesla is another example of how artificial intelligence can be used to revolutionize an industry. The electric car company uses the intelligent machine for its autonomous driving system, Tesla Autopilot. Using a combination of sensors, radar and cameras, as well as deep learning to interpret the data, Tesla Autopilot is able to automatically pilot the car in a wide range of driving situations.

Microsoft has also embraced AI at all levels of its organization. The company uses intelligent machines to improve its products, including its Windows operating system and Office productivity suite. Microsoft has also developed a series of AI tools for developers, such as Azure Machine Learning, which enables developers to easily create and deploy machine learning models.

DeepMind the subsidiary of Alphabet, Google's parent company, DeepMind has been making waves in the AI world with its deep learning algorithms. Its AlphaGo system made headlines in 2016 by beating a world champion in the game of Go, a feat considered a major milestone in the development of AI. Since then, DeepMind has continued to push the boundaries of intelligent machines, notably by applying deep learning to basic science problems such as protein structure prediction.

These examples show just how integrated AI is across a wide range of industries and products. Whether to improve efficiency, optimize processes, offer personalized recommendations or even revolutionize entire sectors, artificial intelligence has become an invaluable tool for 21st century businesses.

AI in the public sector:

The public sector has also begun to embrace AI. Governments are using AI to improve public services, optimize operations and make data-driven decisions. For example, public health departments can use AI to predict disease outbreaks, optimize resource allocation and improve patient care.

However, the use of AI by the public sector also presents challenges. Issues of fairness, transparency and accountability are of major importance. For example, how can we ensure that intelligent machine systems do not introduce bias into decision-making? How can we guarantee transparency in government use of AI? Who is responsible when artificial intelligence makes a mistake?

In short, the adoption of AI by businesses and institutions is growing rapidly, offering enormous benefits, but also new challenges. As we continue to explore and innovate in the field of AI, it's essential to consider these issues and work to create AI systems that are not only effective, but also fair, transparent and accountable.

AI and society:

From concept to dominant force in technological innovation, artificial intelligence has travelled a tumultuous path, passing through various phases of public acceptance, rejection and curiosity. Once considered a science-fiction enigma, the presence of and interaction with AI is now deeply rooted in the daily reality of millions, if not billions, of people around the world. This transition cannot be attributed solely to the speed of technological evolution, but also to a marked and ongoing change in society's perception and acceptance of artificial intelligence. Let's take a closer look at how we have moved from initial skepticism and feelings of fear, even rejection, to growing acceptance, and even a desire to integrate AI into various aspects of our lives.

The advent of the intelligent machine has been accompanied by a wave of fascination and skepticism. The first decades of its development were marked by ambitious promises, but also by fears, eliciting reactions ranging from unbridled enthusiasm to fears of a dystopian future controlled by machines. This has been exacerbated by often sensationalist media and film portrayals of AI, which have played a significant role in shaping public opinion.

However, as AI-based technologies began to infiltrate various aspects of our daily lives - from personal assistants like Siri and Alexa, to product recommendations on e-commerce platforms, to spam filtering algorithms - artificial intelligence became less of an abstraction and more of a concrete reality for people. The public has begun to see AI not as a distant futuristic concept, but as a practical and useful tool that can make everyday life easier.

What's more, AI's impact on the economy has also played a major role in its acceptance. With the intelligent machine creating new industries and transforming existing ones, from agriculture and healthcare to automotive and financial services, people have begun to recognize its economic potential and the opportunities it can offer.

Nevertheless, as the acceptance and integration of the intelligent machine into society continues to broaden, it is essential to remain aware of the ethical challenges and dilemmas that this technology can raise. Questions of privacy, security, fairness and accountability remain major concerns, and require sustained attention from researchers, policymakers and the general public. Let's take a closer look at how initial skepticism has given way to acceptance, and how AI is increasingly integrated into our daily lives.

Public perception of AI:

At the dawn of artificial intelligence, skepticism prevailed. AI was seen as a laboratory curiosity, interesting but far from applicable in real life. Fears persisted, fueled by dystopian science-fiction scenarios of machines taking over humanity.

With the development of more tangible and useful technologies, this perception has begun to change. Voice assistants like Siri and Alexa appeared in homes, making AI tangible and practical. Recommendation algorithms, used by platforms like Netflix or Amazon, have shown they can understand our preferences, suggesting movies to watch or products to buy. Autonomous cars, while still in development, have demonstrated the potential of artificial intelligence to revolutionize transportation.

Integrating AI into everyday life

Today, the intelligent machine is integrating itself into our daily lives at an unprecedented pace. Intelligent machine-based personal assistants help us manage our schedules, remind us of important tasks, and even entertain us with jokes or anecdotes. E-learning platforms use AI to tailor content to students' individual needs, promoting more personalized learning. Even in the healthcare sector, artificial intelligence is making significant inroads, with algorithms capable of analyzing the results of medical tests or predicting the risks of certain diseases.

The future looks bright, with AI poised to transform even more areas. Smart cities, using artificial intelligence to manage infrastructure and improve quality of life, are becoming a reality. The intelligent machine could also play an increasingly important role in the fight against climate change, helping to optimize the use of resources and develop sustainable technologies.

Socio-cultural impacts of the growing adoption of AI

The growing adoption of artificial intelligence is having a profound impact on our society and culture. Communication and social interaction are being transformed, with more and more conversations and transactions taking place via intelligent machine interfaces. The intelligent machine is redefining our notions of work and productivity, with automation replacing certain tasks and creating new opportunities. AI is even having an impact on art and creativity, with AI-generated artworks being sold in galleries and museums.

However, these transformations are not without their challenges. Questions of ethics and responsibility are at the forefront, with concerns about privacy, security, fairness and transparency. These challenges require serious attention and commitment from all players in society: artificial intelligence developers, legislators, educators and citizens.

The intelligent machine has come a long way, from laboratory curiosity to everyday companion. Initial skepticism has given way to growing acceptance, and AI is becoming increasingly integrated into our lives. The impacts are profound, and will transform our society and culture in lasting ways. However, we must remain vigilant to the challenges posed by this integration, and ensure that artificial intelligence is used ethically and for the benefit of all.

-4-

Why learn to use AI properly?

"Artificial intelligence will either be the best or the worst thing that ever happened to us."

Stephen Hawking

Learn how to interact effectively with AI

Centuries ago, the creation of the wheel changed the way we travel and transport goods, giving rise to a world in constant evolution. Today, we are witnessing another technological revolution, that of artificial intelligence, which promises to reshape our lives and work in equally significant ways. In this chapter, we explore the need for a partnership between man and machine to maximize the potential of this new technological era.

The complementary roles of man and AI

The first question to ask is how humans and machines can work together productively. By recognizing the distinct strengths of each party, we can design a complementary partnership.

Machines, for example, are excellent at processing large quantities of data at incredible speed. Take the field of healthcare: machine learning algorithms can analyze thousands of medical images in a matter of minutes, far surpassing human capacity. This means that diseases such as cancer can be detected earlier and more accurately.

However, AI does not replace the important role of the doctor. Humans possess a contextual understanding and empathy that intelligent machines still lack. A doctor can interpret AI results, take into account the patient's preferences and fears, and explain the results in a reassuring and understandable way. In this way, AI and doctors work together to provide better care.

Perspectives on the man-machine partnership

This man-machine partnership is important in many other fields. Take driving, for example. With the advent of autonomous cars, AI is able to process a wealth of data in real time to drive a car more safely and efficiently. However, there will always be situations where human judgment is required, such as when complex ethical decisions need to be made in a fraction of a second. The human-machine partnership can also stimulate creativity. For example, in the field of music, AI tools such as OpenAI's MuseNet can generate new melodies, but it is the human artist who interprets, organizes and gives meaning to these musical ideas, creating a unique work of art.

Preparing the company for this new dynamic

It is essential to prepare our society for this new dynamic of man-machine partnership. This means reformulating our education system to include digital skills and a basic understanding of artificial intelligence from an early age. We must also insist on the development of essential human skills such as critical thinking, creativity, empathy and ethics, which are complementary to AI.

In addition, we need to consider regulations to ensure that this partnership is fair and ethical. For example, who is responsible when an autonomous car is involved in an accident? How can we ensure that artificial intelligence systems respect users' privacy? These are major questions that require careful thought.

The advent of artificial intelligence offers us an unprecedented opportunity to reshape our world. By forging this partnership, we can maximize the potential of the intelligent machine while preserving what makes us deeply human. The journey will be complex and fraught with challenges, but the potential benefits are immense. It's time to embrace this new era of collaboration between man and machine.

The importance of effective dialogue with AI

As artificial intelligence systems such as ChatGPT develop and become more widespread, it becomes essential to learn how to interact with them effectively. This is particularly true in the field of language models, where an effective "prompt" - i.e. a well-formulated query or stimulus - can make all the difference in terms of the results obtained. This chapter explores why an effective prompt is essential, the foundations of communication with language models, and the current limits of the intelligent machine in understanding human language.

Why an effective Prompt is essential

AI language models, such as ChatGPT, are designed to generate responses based on the nature and structure of the prompt you give them. In other words, the quality of the response you get depends directly on the quality of your prompt. For example, if you ask ChatGPT to give you "advice on how to succeed in business", you might get a very general response, as the query is broad and could be interpreted in many different ways. However, if you specify your prompt to say "Give me tips on how to improve customer service in an Italian restaurant", ChatGPT will be able to generate a much more precise and useful response.

The Foundations of Communication with AI Language Models

Communicating with an AI language model requires a slightly different approach than you would with a human. Here are some key principles to keep in mind:

Precision: Language models respond literally. So it's important to be as precise as possible in your phrasing. For example, if you ask "What's the best book?", the answer could be very subjective. On the other hand, if you ask "What's the best-selling book in 2023?", the AI can provide a more objective answer.

Contextualization: Providing the right context can help elicit a more appropriate response. For example, rather than asking, "How do you make a pie?", you could ask, "How do you make an apple pie from scratch for four people?".

Formatting: Feel free to specify the format you want for the answer. For example, if you want a list of book recommendations, you can specify it by saying: "List five popular science fiction books released in 2023".

AI's limits in understanding human language

Despite remarkable progress in the field of artificial intelligence, it's important to recognize that AI language models still have significant limitations in understanding human language. For example, they don't really understand context in the same way that a human would. If you tell ChatGPT that "it's literally cold outside", it won't understand that you mean it's very cold - it will literally interpret that it's "cold" outside.

Similarly, language models cannot understand emotion or intonation in the same way as humans. For example, if you type "That's amazing!", the AI can't discern whether you're genuinely amazed or being bitingly sarcastic.

Finally, it's important to note that AI language models, while impressive, don't "think" or "understand" in the human sense. They generate responses based on patterns in the data on which they have been trained, not on genuine understanding or awareness.

Effective interaction with AI language models relies on understanding these limitations and formulating prompts that are clear, precise and appropriate. When done well, this interaction can unlock impressive potential, enabling these AI tools to provide useful information, automate complex tasks and even stimulate human creativity.

Building a relationship of trust with AI

At the dawn of this revolutionary technological era, we find ourselves at a crossroads, faced with the daunting task of integrating artificial intelligence into the very fabric of our daily lives. AI has the potential to transform our world in ways barely imaginable just a few decades ago. However, to fully realize and exploit this potential, it is essential that we learn to build a relationship of trust with these AI systems. This trust is not just limited to the ability of AI to function as intended, but also encompasses deeper considerations related to transparency, ethics, personal data protection, and the recognition and mitigation of potential biases.

Understanding how AI works, what its limitations are and how it arrives at its conclusions are key aspects of intelligent machine transparency. For many users, artificial intelligence algorithms are often perceived as "black boxes", producing results without giving any clear indication of how these results were obtained. To build a genuine relationship of trust, it is necessary to develop methods that make these processes more transparent and comprehensible to everyone, from non-technical users to political decision-makers.

AI systems, although designed by humans, have no intrinsic moral or ethical value system. It's up to us to ensure that these systems are used ethically and responsibly, respect human rights, promote fairness and justice, and avoid causing unjustified harm.

As we make increasing use of the intelligent machine in our lives, we generate huge amounts of data that can be used to power these systems. It's essential that we understand how our data is used, who has access to it, and how we can control and protect this information.

Developing transparent and ethical AI

Transparency and ethics are at the heart of any trusting relationship. In the context of AI, transparency means that the decision-making processes of artificial intelligence are open to scrutiny and can be understood by users. For example, a transparent AI could provide a natural language explanation of how it arrived at a particular conclusion or a specific recommendation.

Take, for example, an AI system used to evaluate loan applications. A transparent AI might explain that it recommended rejection of a loan application because the applicant had a credit score below the threshold value defined by the bank, already had several loans outstanding, and did not have a stable income. This contrasts with an opaque artificial intelligence, which might simply reject the application without providing an explanation.

Ethics, on the other hand, implies that AI is designed and used in a way that respects users' fundamental values and rights. This could involve, for example, ensuring that the intelligent machine does not discriminate against certain groups of users, or guaranteeing that artificial intelligence respects users' privacy by collecting and using personal data only appropriately and with the user's consent.

Understanding and managing AI bias

All artificial intelligence systems are likely to be affected by biases, which can be introduced at various stages of the AI development process, for example during data collection, when training the intelligent machine, or even when using the AI. It is therefore essential to understand these biases and know how to manage them.

Let's take the example of an artificial intelligence system used for recruitment. If the training data used to develop the artificial intelligence is biased, for example if it contains mainly examples of successful male candidates, then the artificial intelligence could develop a bias in favor of male candidates. To manage this bias, it is important to ensure that the training data is representative of the diversity of potential candidates. In addition, it may be necessary to regularly test the AI for any bias, and correct the intelligent machine model if necessary.

The role of AI in protecting personal data

Finally, the protection of personal data is another key aspect of building a relationship of trust with artificial intelligence. AI systems often depend on vast amounts of data, including personal data, to operate effectively. It is therefore essential that these systems are designed and used in a way that respects users' privacy and protects their personal data.

For example, an AI system could be used to recommend products to a user based on their purchase history. To protect the user's privacy, the smart machine could be designed to retain only the minimum information needed to make recommendations, to anonymize the user's data so that it cannot be linked to the user, and to allow the user to control what data is collected and how it is used.

In short, building a relationship of trust with AI means understanding and managing these issues. By developing a transparent and ethical intelligent machine, by understanding and managing the biases of artificial intelligence, and by respecting the protection of personal data, we can use AI effectively and responsibly.

AI education:

In a world where artificial intelligence is revolutionizing many fields, from medicine to education to transportation, understanding and knowing how to use this technology is becoming a fundamental skill for every individual. In this chapter, we'll explore why education in artificial intelligence is essential for our future, how educational programs adapt to all ages, and why ongoing AI training is necessary for professionals.

Why AI education is essential for our future

It's important to recognize that AI is not a technology of the future, but of the present. Increasingly, our jobs, our leisure activities and even our social interactions are affected or mediated by artificial intelligence. For example, personalized recommendations on

Netflix are generated by AI, as are search results on Google or targeted ads on Facebook. The autonomous car that could drive you tomorrow? It's also the fruit of intelligent machines.

Yet, despite this ubiquity, the majority of people have a limited understanding of AI and how it works. This gap represents an obstacle not only to employment and informed engagement in a digital world, but also to making political and ethical decisions about AI. For example, how can we discuss the regulation of artificial intelligence in an informed way if we don't understand what intelligent machines can and cannot do?

It is therefore essential to educate the public about artificial intelligence - not only to enable individuals to reap its benefits, but also to enable them to understand the wider implications of its use.

AI education programs for all ages

Fortunately, more and more initiatives are seeking to integrate AI education into school curricula for all ages. In elementary school, for example, students can be introduced to the intelligent machine through simple projects, such as programming a robot to follow a path or creating a simple chatbot. These projects enable students to understand the basic concepts of artificial intelligence while developing their logical thinking and creativity.

At secondary level, students can deepen their understanding of AI by learning more advanced programming languages and exploring concepts such as machine learning and natural language processing. They can also start thinking about the ethical and social implications of artificial intelligence, debating topics such as automating work or data privacy.

In higher education, students can choose to specialize in AI-related fields such as computer science, robotics or data science. However, even for those who do not specialize in these fields, a basic understanding of artificial intelligence is increasingly necessary. Consequently, many universities offer AI courses for non-specialists, covering both the technical aspects and the social implications of artificial intelligence.

AI training for professionals

However, AI education doesn't stop at school or university. In a world where the intelligent machine is evolving rapidly, continuing education is essential to stay up to date. This is especially true for professionals whose jobs are directly impacted by AI, such as software developers, data analysts or digital marketers.

Fortunately, there are plenty of resources for continuing education in artificial intelligence. Online courses, such as those offered by Coursera or edX, allow professionals to learn at their own pace and on their own schedule. Conferences and workshops, such as those organized by NeurIPS or OpenAI, offer opportunities for networking and discovering the latest AI research.

What's more, many companies recognize the importance of ongoing AI training and offer in-house training to their employees. For example, Google has developed an AI training program for its employees, covering everything from machine learning to AI ethics.

AI can help shape our future

Artificial Intelligence is a powerful tool that offers many benefits for everyday life. From improving productivity to promoting individual well-being and increasing accessibility, AI plays an important role in empowering individuals and creating new opportunities for all.

The Benefits of AI for Everyday Life

On a daily basis, artificial intelligence makes our lives easier in many ways, often without us even being aware of it. For example, when you use a GPS navigation service like Google Maps, AI algorithms are at work to analyze real-time data, predict traffic, and provide you with the fastest route. If you use a voice assistant like Alexa or Siri, it's artificial intelligence that understands your voice, interprets your query, and gives you a relevant response.

Another example is the recommendation system used by streaming platforms such as Netflix or Spotify. AI analyzes your preferences and past listening or viewing behavior to suggest new content that might interest you. These examples show how artificial intelligence is already integrated into our daily lives, making many aspects of our lives more efficient and personalized.

How AI Can Improve Productivity and Individual Well-Being

Beyond convenience, artificial intelligence can also have a significant positive impact on our individual productivity and well-being. In terms of productivity, AI tools can help automate routine tasks and organize our days. For example, AI apps like Todoist or Google Tasks can help us manage our to-do lists, recommending priorities based on our past behavior. Intelligent machine tools can also automate more complex tasks, such as report writing or data analysis, freeing up time for more creative and rewarding tasks.

When it comes to individual well-being, AI can play a role in a variety of areas, from sleep to mental health. Sleep tracking apps use AI to analyze sleep data and provide personalized advice to improve sleep quality. Mental health apps, such as Woebot, use

AI to provide personalized cognitive-behavioral therapies, helping users manage stress and anxiety.

AI and Accessibility: Providing Opportunities for All

AI also has the potential to dramatically increase accessibility and offer opportunities to those who were previously marginalized or excluded. For example, AI technologies can help visually impaired or blind people navigate the world. Applications such as Microsoft's Seeing AI use computer vision to describe the environment, read text or recognize faces, offering users greater autonomy.

In education, artificial intelligence can help personalize learning, adapting teaching materials and methods to the specific needs of each student. Tools like Duolingo use AI to tailor language lessons to each user's progress, which can help increase learning engagement and effectiveness.

It can offer significant benefits for everyday life, improve productivity and individual well-being, and increase accessibility for all. As individuals, it's important to understand these opportunities and exploit them to improve our lives and those around us.

AI as an Agent of Change

Artificial Intelligence has become an agent of change, reshaping many aspects of human life, from economic and social systems to our interaction with the world around us. It has the potential to transform society in unprecedented ways and solve pressing global problems such as climate change, education challenges and health crises. However, like any disruptive technology, AI also presents challenges that need to be carefully addressed.

AI-induced societal transformations

AI has introduced substantial societal transformations in a variety of sectors. In the world of work, for example, artificial intelligence has automated many tasks once carried out by humans, from self-service checkouts in supermarkets to the use of Chatbots for customer service. This has changed the nature of the jobs available and required new skills.

What's more, artificial intelligence has improved decision-making in many fields. Insurance companies use AI to predict risks and adjust rates, governments use it to optimize public services, and businesses of all sizes rely on AI to analyze market trends and make strategic decisions.

AI as a tool for tackling global challenges

Climate change: AI algorithms can help model and predict climate change, enabling scientists and decision-makers to develop more effective strategies to mitigate impacts. For example, Google uses AI to optimize energy consumption in its data centers, thereby reducing their carbon footprint.

Education: artificial intelligence can offer personalized solutions to learners, adapting to their learning pace and preferences. Artificial intelligence-based learning applications like Duolingo use these techniques to offer personalized language lessons to each user.

Healthcare: artificial intelligence can help predict epidemics, develop new drugs, improve diagnosis and personalize treatment. One example is IBM's Watson AI system, which helps doctors diagnose and treat cancer.

Facing the challenges of AI

However, AI also presents challenges that need to be addressed. One of the most notable is the risk of unemployment due to automation. Workers in automated sectors need to be trained in new skills to remain employable. There are also data privacy and security issues, as AI relies on huge amounts of data, often personal. What's more, AI can perpetuate and even amplify existing biases if trained on biased data.

To manage these challenges, it is necessary to put in place appropriate policies, encourage transparency and fairness in the development of artificial intelligence, and educate the public about the implications of AI.

AI is a powerful agent of change, offering immense opportunities while posing significant challenges. By understanding these aspects, we can shape a future where artificial intelligence is used for the benefit of all.

Making AI thrive in our Lives: A Practical Guide

In a world where technology is becoming increasingly integrated into our daily lives, it's essential to learn how to use artificial intelligence to achieve our personal and professional goals. This chapter offers a practical guide to integrating AI into our daily lives and keeping abreast of the latest advances.

Using AI to achieve your personal and professional goals

AI offers a range of possibilities for achieving personal and professional goals. For example, consider a common personal goal: improving one's physical health. AI-based fitness applications can help achieve this goal by providing personalized training programs, tracking progress and adapting exercises according to the user's performance and reactions.

In the professional arena, a sales manager looking to increase team productivity might use AI software for data analysis. These tools can identify trends and patterns in sales, suggest improvement strategies based on past patterns and even predict future trends, enabling the team to make informed, proactive decisions.

Best Practices for Integrating AI into Everyday Life

To effectively integrate artificial intelligence into our daily lives, it's important to understand its capabilities and limitations. Here are some best practices:

Use AI to automate repetitive tasks: many AI tools can handle routine tasks, leaving you more time to focus on more important tasks. For example, a virtual assistant like Alexa can manage your calendar, remind you of appointments, and even order groceries online.

Be aware of privacy and security issues: make sure you understand the privacy and security settings of the smart machine tools you use. Be aware of what data you're sharing and how it's being used and stored.

Learn to ask the right questions: as with any tool, the successful use of AI depends largely on how you use it. Learning how to formulate queries and instructions effectively can greatly improve the quality of the results you get from artificial intelligence.

How can I keep abreast of the latest advances in AI?

The field of artificial intelligence is in a constant state of flux, evolving at a speed that defies comprehension. New discoveries and revolutionary applications emerge almost daily, constantly pushing back the boundaries of what's possible. In this whirlwind of innovation, keeping abreast of the latest advances is both a vital and Herculean task, whether for researchers, engineers, entrepreneurs, policy-makers or simply technology enthusiasts. For those looking to make their way through this labyrinth of information, here are a few strategies that may prove useful:

Keeping up with the latest scientific journals is essential. Research articles are the front line in the advancement of knowledge, offering direct visibility on the most recent advances in the field. Journals such as "Nature Machine Intelligence", "The Journal of Artificial Intelligence Research", or "IEEE Transactions on Neural Networks and Learning Systems" are examples of recognized and respected sources. Membership of AI-related professional or academic organizations can provide access to valuable resources.

Organizations such as the Association for the Advancement of Artificial Intelligence (AAAI) or the IEEE Computational Intelligence Society offer seminars, conferences and newsletters that can help keep you up to date with current advances.

Conferences and workshops are another way of keeping up to date. These events are not only platforms for presenting the latest research, but also opportunities for networking and collaboration. Conferences like NeurIPS, ICML, and AAAI are internationally renowned and attract leading AI researchers. Above all, I recommend subscribing to newsletters, Youtube channels and specialized blogs, which can provide regular analysis of trends and developments. Resources such as the MIT Technology Review, Import AI's The Artificial Intelligence Newsletter or the OpenAI blog are valuable sources of regular information.

Don't neglect social media in this area-platforms like Twitter, LinkedIn and GitHub can be excellent sources of information, as many researchers, engineers and companies regularly share updates on their work.

Staying up to date on the latest advances in AI is no easy task, given the speed at which the field is evolving. However, by combining a variety of strategies - from reading academic journals to attending conferences, joining professional organizations and engaging on social media - it is possible to stay up-to-date in this exciting and constantly evolving field. Please let me know if you have any discoveries, feedback or ideas in this area at contact@ebook-corp.com .

AI and the Future: Perspectives and Reflections

Artificial intelligence is becoming a transformative force in almost every aspect of our daily lives, and this movement shows no signs of slowing down. On the contrary, as we move towards an increasingly digitized future, the role of artificial intelligence is likely to become even more central. In this section, we look at some of the predictions for the future of AI, how we can prepare for a future dominated by artificial intelligence, and the role we, as individuals, can play in shaping that future.

Predictions on the Future of AI

It's hard to predict exactly how artificial intelligence will evolve in the future, but there are some clear trends emerging. First and foremost, we should expect AI to become increasingly ubiquitous. Whether in autonomous cars, intelligent personal assistants, healthcare systems, education or the infrastructure of our cities, artificial intelligence is likely to play an increasingly important role.

In healthcare, for example, AI could revolutionize the way we diagnose and treat disease. Machine learning algorithms are already capable of detecting abnormalities on X-rays and scans with an accuracy equivalent to or better than that of human radiologists. In the future, these technologies could be deployed on a large scale, enabling diseases to be diagnosed more quickly and accurately, and thus improving outcomes for patients.

How to prepare for an AI-driven future

To prepare for an AI-dominated future, it's important to gain a basic understanding of what artificial intelligence is and how it works. This doesn't necessarily mean that everyone needs to become an AI expert, but rather that we all need to have some knowledge of the basics.

We should all understand that AI works by identifying patterns in data, and using these patterns to make predictions or decisions. This means that AI performance is strongly influenced by the quality of the data it receives. Understanding this principle can help us interpret the recommendations made by AI, and understand why it can sometimes get it wrong.

What's more, in an AI-dominated future, it will be important to have skills that complement those of artificial intelligence. Problem-solving, creativity and critical thinking skills will still be valuable, even in a world where AI is ubiquitous.

The Role of the Individual in Shaping the Future of AI

Finally, it's important to note that we, as individuals, have a role to play in shaping the future of AI. We can influence the direction AI takes by expressing our preferences and concerns, whether as consumers, as workers, or as citizens.

If we're concerned about the impact of artificial intelligence on employment, for example, we can choose to support companies that use AI responsibly, invest in training their employees to help them adapt to the AI era, and commit to a just transition to a digital economy.

The future of artificial intelligence is in our hands, and it's up to us to educate ourselves, prepare ourselves and become actively involved in AI debates to ensure that this technology is used in a way that benefits everyone, and not just a few of the richest or most powerful. Be careful, however, to see and understand that AI is now inevitable in its development, given that the technology exists, and stopping its development would only develop misuse by criminals who themselves do not respect the law, but would place too many constraints on developing the right versions of intelligent machines to counteract them and ensure us of a better future.

-5-

The power of the swift

"AI is probably the greatest event in human history. It will be bigger than the invention of fire or electricity."

Elon Musk

Exploring the fascinating world of artificial intelligence often leads us to delve into complex, technological details. However, there is a fundamental and often underestimated component of this interaction: prompts. Prompts are more than just an interface between the user and the AI, they play a decisive role in how the AI understands and reacts to our queries. In this paper, we'll explore the nature of prompts, how they work and their crucial importance in the world of AI.

The term "prompt" is derived from the Latin "promptus", meaning "ready for use". In the context of AI, a prompt is an instruction or request that we pass on to a language model in order to elicit a response. Whether it's a simple question like "What's the weather like today?" or a more complex task like "Write an article on the history of the French Revolution", every interaction we undertake with AI is initiated by a prompt. Every question we ask, every task we assign, is a prompt that sets the tone for the interaction with the language model.

Language models, such as ChatGPT, are sophisticated computer systems that have been trained on billions of words of text. As they train, these models learn to predict the next word in a sentence based on the words that preceded it. When we present a prompt to ChatGPT, we provide it with the starting point of a sentence and, from there, it uses what it has learned during its training to generate a sequence. If we provide the AI with the prompt "Once upon a time", it might generate a response such as "Once upon a time there was a king who lived in a faraway kingdom". This response is produced thanks to its ability to predict what might logically follow "Once upon a time" in a sentence.

Prompts play an essential role for two main reasons. Firstly, they are our main means of communication with artificial intelligence. It's thanks to prompts that we can interrogate ChatGPT, ask it to write text for us, and much more. On the other hand, the quality of the prompt can have a significant impact on the quality of the response. A well-formulated prompt can lead to a precise, detailed and useful response, whereas a poorly formulated prompt can result in a vague, incorrect or useless answer. Thus, mastering the art of formulating prompts is an essential skill for optimizing the effective use of AI.

Therefore, understanding what a prompt is, how it works and its importance is an essential step towards becoming an expert in prompt formulation. In the following chapters, we'll explore these concepts in greater depth, and explore advanced techniques for formulating prompts.

In the field of AI, prompts play a central role. These triggers or requests for information that you present to the AI are the fuel that powers the text generation engine. They provide the initial context the model needs to generate an appropriate response. The choice of prompt can have a significant impact on the quality of the response generated by the AI. A well-formulated prompt can help the model produce accurate, relevant and creative responses, while an imprecise or vague prompt can result in less useful answers. Therefore, mastering the art of prompt formulation is a valuable skill for working effectively with AI-based language models.

Understanding prompts

Prompts are at the heart of the way we interact with language models such as ChatGPT. Indeed, the dialogue between man and machine revolves around those carefully worded instructions or well-posed questions that serve as a guide to our intelligent machines. Prompts, in their essence, are like the beacons of a lighthouse, directing the vast oceans of artificial intelligence towards the shores of our specific needs. But to navigate with ease and efficiency, it's imperative to understand in depth the nature and operation of prompts.

Prompts, in their simplest expression, are requests or instructions that we address to a language model, indicating what we expect it to do. This directive may be a question to be answered, a sentence to be completed, a topic to be developed or even a writing style to be imitated. It's thanks to these prompts that language models are able to generate relevant, coherent and often surprisingly humanized responses.

However, the art of writing prompts goes beyond simply formulating a question or instruction. It's about creating a clear path for the model to follow, while taking into account the inherent characteristics of the model in question. Language models like ChatGPT have no knowledge or understanding of the real world, they simply generate text based on what they have "learned" when training on huge text datasets. Therefore, an effective prompt must take this fundamental limitation into account.

What's more, understanding how to structure and refine prompts can also help us obtain more precise and relevant responses. Prompt length, level of detail or specificity, and even tone can all influence the response generated by the language model.

In their simplest form, prompts are the instructions or questions we give to a language model to tell it what we want it to do. But to really master the art of writing prompts, it's essential to understand more deeply what they are and how they work.

What is a prompt?

A prompt, a term frequently used in the context of artificial intelligence, is essentially an instruction or request we make to a language model to tell it what task it should perform. Whether it's asking a question, requesting text generation on a specific topic, or prompting the model to continue a story, every interaction with the model is initiated by a prompt.

To understand this in greater depth, let's look at a few examples. If we ask the question "What's the weather like today?" to a language model such as ChatGPT, this question acts as a prompt. It serves to guide the AI's response, prompting it to provide information about the current weather. Similarly, if we ask ChatGPT to "Write an article on the history of the French Revolution", this request also acts as a prompt, this time guiding the AI to produce a detailed text article on the specified topic. In other words, every time we give an instruction to the AI, whether to ask a question, write a text or perform some other task, we give a prompt. The prompt also serves to define the direction and context of the response. A well-formulated prompt can help to obtain more precise, relevant and useful answers. For example, a vague prompt like "Tell me something" could lead to a wide variety of responses, as the model has a very wide response space. On the other hand, a more specific prompt like "Explain the theory of relativity to me" would give the model a clear direction and lead to a much more focused and informative response.

How do prompts work?

Language models like ChatGPT are trained on billions of words of text. During training, they learn to predict the next word in a sentence based on the words that preceded it. When we give the AI a prompt, we're essentially giving it the start of a sentence, and it uses what it's learned in training to generate what comes next. If we give ChatGPT the prompt "Once upon a time", it might generate a response like "Once upon a time there was a king who lived in a faraway kingdom". It generates this response by using its training to predict what might logically follow "Once upon a time" in a sentence.

Why are prompts important?

Prompts are essential for two main reasons. Firstly, they are the primary means by which we communicate with ChatGPT. It's thanks to prompts that we're able to ask the AI questions, have it write text for us, and more.

Secondly, the quality of the prompt has a significant impact on the quality of the response. A well-written prompt can help produce an accurate, detailed and useful response, whereas a poorly-written prompt can lead to a vague, incorrect or useless response. In other words, mastering the art of prompt writing is essential to maximizing the effectiveness of ChatGPT.

In short, understanding what prompts are and how they work is the essential first step to becoming an expert at writing prompts. In future chapters, we'll delve even deeper into these concepts and explore advanced techniques for writing prompts.

The role of prompts in AI

Prompts play a major role in the operation of AI-based language models such as OpenAI's GPT-3 and GPT-4. Prompts are the triggers, primers or requests for information that you present to the AI. They provide the initial context the model needs to generate an appropriate response.

The prompt can be as simple as a single question ("What's the weather like today?") or as complex as a sequence of sentences providing detailed context and precise instructions. Language models process these prompts and generate an output text sequence that is, in theory, a coherent and relevant continuation of the input text.

The choice of prompt can have a significant impact on the quality of the response generated by artificial intelligence. A good prompt can help the model produce accurate, relevant and creative responses, while an imprecise or vague prompt can result in less useful answers. Therefore, mastering the art of prompt formulation is a valuable skill for working effectively with AI language models.

Prompts also serve to guide the AI on the tone, style and format of the desired response. A prompt that asks ChatGPT to "summarize an article as if you were writing it for five-year-olds" will give a very different response from a prompt that asks the AI to "summarize the article in formal academic language". In more advanced applications, prompts can be used to control language models more finely. For example, by providing a prompt that includes a series of previous questions and answers, a language model can be designed to maintain a longer, more coherent conversation thread. They serve as a starting point for interactions with AI, provide a framework for AI-generated responses, and can help refine and direct AI creativity and ingenuity in productive and useful ways.

Define result expectations

Defining your expectations for the outcome of a prompt is a major but often overlooked step in the process of creating effective AI prompts. It's your vision of the desired outcome that drives your prompt formulation, guides your adjustments and allows you to evaluate the success of your prompt. Before writing a prompt, ask yourself, "What is the specific result I want from AI?"

Your answer can be as simple as "I want AI to give me a list of all the American presidents" or as complex as "I want AI to create a suspenseful science fiction story that explores the ethical implications of genetic engineering". The clearer and more specific your expectations, the easier it will be to create a prompt that achieves the desired result.

When defining your expectations, it's important to consider the nature of the language model you're using. Models like GPT-3 and GPT-4 are incredibly powerful and capable of generating a wide range of creative responses. However, they have their limitations. They can't access information in real time, they don't understand context the way humans do, and they're not infallible when it comes to accuracy. Consequently, your expectations must be realistic, given the model's capabilities and limitations.

Once you've defined your expectations, you can start formulating your prompt. The key to getting the desired result is to make your prompt as specific and detailed as possible. If you want a list of American presidents, make that clear in your prompt. If you want a science fiction story, give the AI as much detail as possible about the kind of story you want.

It's also useful to formulate your prompt in such a way as to guide the artificial intelligence towards the type of answer you want. If you want a detailed answer, you can use phrases like "Explain in detail" or "Give a complete answer". If you want a concise answer, you can use phrases like "Answer in one sentence" or "Give a short answer".

Once you've received a response from ChatGPT, evaluate it against your expectations. Did the AI produce the result you wanted? If not, what adjustments can you make to your prompt to achieve a better result? This evaluation and adjustment is an essential part of the prompt creation process and will help you hone your prompt creation skills.

By clearly defining your result expectations, formulating specific and detailed prompts, and evaluating and adjusting your prompts according to these expectations, you can maximize the probability of obtaining the desired results from your AI prompts.

-6-

Foundations of prompt engineering

"The question is not whether artificial intelligence will be smarter than humans, but when."

Ray Kurzweil

The information age has seen the emergence of increasingly sophisticated technologies for processing and understanding human language. These technologies, known as language models, have become an essential part of our daily interaction with machines, powering applications ranging from voice assistants to search engines and machine translation tools.

Language models are the fruit of decades of research in artificial intelligence, machine learning and computational linguistics. They reflect our quest to create machines capable of understanding and generating human language in a natural and meaningful way. In the following paragraphs, we will explore the mechanics of language models in depth, starting with an overview of what they are and how they work, and then looking at two types of language model: n-gram-based models and neural network-based models.

We'll be looking at the Transformer and GPT models, which are at the forefront of this technology, powering cutting-edge text generation systems such as ChatGPT.

How AI interprets prompts

Before we delve into the details of writing prompts, we need to understand how a machine learning model, such as GPT-3 or GPT-4, interprets these prompts. This understanding is the key to determining how to formulate effective prompts that achieve the desired results.

GPT, which stands for "Generative Pretrained Transformer", is a type of language model based on transformers. Transformers are neural network architectures that use self-attention, a mechanism that allows the model to weight the importance of different words or phrases when generating a response.

When you give GPT a prompt, it uses this prompt as a starting point for generating text. The model "reads" the prompt you've provided, and from there generates a sequence of words that it thinks is the most likely continuation of that prompt. It does this using the knowledge it has gained from training on billions of sentences and texts.

In particular, the model examines each word in the prompt in context and attempts to predict the next word based on the probability of that word appearing after the previous words. This process is repeated at each stage until the model reaches a certain text length or generates an end-of-sentence token, whichever comes first.

It's important to note that GPT doesn't have a semantic or contextual understanding of the world in the same way as a human being. It doesn't really understand what a "cat" or an "apple" is, beyond what its training patterns have shown it. It simply generates text on the basis of probabilities, without any real understanding or awareness of what it is "saying".

Consequently, the art of writing prompts often involves carefully guiding the template to achieve the desired results. This may mean being more specific in your prompts, using a particular wording or format, or spelling out certain instructions to guide the template.

Another important aspect to understand is that models like GPT-3 and GPT-4 are "deterministic". This means that they will produce the same output for the same prompt each time they are run, unless an element of "randomization" or "temperature" is introduced into the generation process.

Temperature" is a parameter you can adjust when running your prompt. A higher temperature will make the model more "creative" and more inclined to take risks, which can lead to more varied, but potentially less consistent responses. A lower temperature, on the other hand, will make the model more conservative in its predictions, which can lead to more predictable and consistent, but potentially less original, responses.

By understanding these concepts, you'll be better equipped to create prompts that maximize AI's strengths and minimize its weaknesses, and you'll be able to formulate prompts that get the results you want.

Understanding the limits of AI

To exploit the full potential of language models like GPT-4, it's essential to understand their limitations. Despite incredible advances in artificial intelligence, these systems still have inherent constraints that can affect the quality and accuracy of their responses. Let's discuss some of these limitations.

Limited, time-sliced knowledge: Language models, such as GPT-4, are trained on large datasets that were compiled at a given point in time. Consequently, they do not have access to real-time information or events that occurred after the date of their last training. ChatGPT, at the time of its last update in September 2021, cannot provide information on events or developments that occurred after that date.

Literal understanding: Although language models are capable of generating impressive, coherent texts, their understanding of the world is literal and based on statistics. They have no awareness or understanding of the real world. As a result, they can sometimes produce answers that, while grammatically correct, may lack common sense or true understanding.

Lack of emotions and subjectivity: AIs have no emotions, opinions or personal feelings. They cannot empathize or understand subtle emotional contexts in the same way as a human being would. Any expression of emotion or opinion is a simulation based on training data, not a true experience or perspective.

Predictions based on training data: The responses generated by language models are based on their training data. Therefore, if this data contains biases or errors, the AI can reproduce them. This can lead to inaccurate, misleading or biased responses.

Uncertainty and ambiguity: Language models can sometimes struggle to handle uncertainty and ambiguity. If a prompt is vague or open to many interpretations, artificial intelligence may not be able to produce a precise or useful answer.

Understanding these limitations is an important step towards becoming a competent prompts engineer. This will enable you to formulate more effective prompts and better interpret AI responses. It's also important to remember that AI is a tool. While it can generate impressive and useful answers, it does not replace human judgment and should not be used as the sole source of information for important or sensitive decisions.

The role of prompts in machine learning

Machine learning is a branch of artificial intelligence that enables machines to learn from data and improve their performance without being explicitly programmed to do so. Prompts play a key role in this process, especially in the context of supervised learning and language models such as GPT-3 or GPT-4.

A prompt is essentially an instruction or question given to a language model to trigger a response. These prompts act as inputs to the model, prompting it to produce a corresponding output. In machine learning terms, prompts are similar to so-called "features" or "independent variables" in a data set. They provide the starting point for the model learning process.

During the training phase, a language model is exposed to millions, if not billions, of prompt-response pairs. These pairs come from vast corpora of text, such as web pages, books and other textual data sources. By observing the relationships between these prompts and the associated responses, the model learns to predict what the most likely response to a given prompt should be. If the prompt is "What is the capital of France?", the model learns that the correct answer is "Paris", as this is the answer that is most often associated with this prompt in the training data. However, unlike a simple question-answer correspondence, language models strive to understand the context and linguistic structure of the prompt, enabling them to generate answers to questions they have never been explicitly trained to answer.

Once the model has been trained, prompts become the means by which users interact with the model. Whether asking the AI to generate a blog post, write an e-mail, or provide an explanation on a particular topic, it's the user's prompt that guides the AI's response. Prompts are essential to machine learning, and in particular to learning language models. They are the engine of learning, providing the basis on which the model learns to understand and generate text. They are also the main interface between the user and the model, enabling interaction that goes far beyond the capabilities of rule-based dialogue systems.

The importance of precision in formulation

Accurate prompt formulation is a key factor when interacting with AI-based language models such as ChatGPT. Because of the way these models are formed, they rely on the information given in the prompt to generate a response. So, the more precise and detailed the prompt, the more relevant and useful the generated response is likely to be.

It's important to understand that these language models have no awareness of the external environment and no access to real-time data. They rely on the patterns, structures and information contained in the large dataset on which they have been trained. Consequently, accurate prompts are necessary to obtain the desired information.

If you ask a language model "What's the best book?", it's likely to generate a general or ambiguous answer, since the notion of "best" is subjective and depends on many factors such as genre, target audience, historical context, etc. On the other hand, if you formulate the prompt in a more precise way, take this example "What's the best science fiction book for teenagers according to literary critics?", the language model has a better chance of producing a specific and relevant answer.

In another case, if you ask an ambiguous question like "Does it fly?", the model can't produce a precise answer because it lacks a clear context. What's supposed to fly? A bird? A plane? A drone? However, if the question is posed as "Can the DJI Mavic Mini drone fly in rainy weather?", the model has all the information it needs to provide a precise answer based on the characteristics and limitations of the drone mentioned. It should be noted that even with precise wording, language models have their limits. They can produce errors, inaccuracies or biased answers depending on the data on which they have been trained. That's why it's always important to treat the answers provided by these models with a degree of skepticism, and to verify them with reliable sources.

Precision in the formulation of prompts is therefore an essential element in navigating effectively in the world of conversational AI. It enables us to make the most of these tools, while remaining aware of their limitations.

Prompt successes and failures

These cases will highlight the challenges inherent in interacting with language models such as ChatGPT, as well as the opportunities for improving the effectiveness of these interactions.

Prompt engineering failures

The first notable failure in prompt engineering comes from the use of questions that are too vague or too open-ended. If you ask a language model "What is life?", you're likely to get a rather vague answer, as the question can be interpreted in many ways. It would be more useful to ask a more precise question, such as "What is life according to biology?" or "What is life according to philosophy?".

Another common failure occurs when users expect AI to understand and respond to implicitly contextual queries, without providing the necessary context. Asking ChatGPT "What did she say?" without providing prior context will result in a meaningless response.

Finally, another typical failure comes from information overload in prompts. Language models like GPT-4 are designed to generate responses based on a limited number of words or tokens, which means that an instruction that is too long can result in a truncated or incomplete response.

Prompt engineering success stories

On the other hand, there are examples of remarkable successes in prompt engineering. Clear, precise wording can lead to very precise results. Asking a language model "What are the symptoms of the flu?" or "Give me a recipe for apple pie" can generate detailed and useful responses.

In addition, prompts that guide the AI towards a certain style or tone can also produce amazing results. GPT-4 with the prompt "Write a poem about spring in the style of William Wordsworth" can generate a poem that captures Wordsworth's romantic tone and deep connection with nature.

Finally, in some cases, open or creative prompts can lead to interesting and unexpected responses. Asking a language model to "Tell a story about a robot who falls in love with a tulip" can generate a creative and unique story.

Prompt engineering is as much an art as a science. Understanding the challenges and opportunities can help us interact more effectively with language models, making the most of their capabilities while navigating around their limitations.

-7-

The tree of thoughts

"Artificial intelligence, deep learning, machine learning - whatever you want to call it, these technologies are going to transform the world."

Mark Cuban

A revolution for language models

Imagine yourself in front of an immense labyrinth, a myriad of paths intertwining before your eyes. Each of these paths represents a potential solution to a given problem. Some lead to a dead end, while others take you closer to the heart of the labyrinth - the solution to the problem. This is the image I'd like to give you to understand the "Tree of Thoughts" concept.

The science of artificial intelligence and, in particular, language models has come a long way, through winding paths, peaks and valleys of intellectual challenge, to get to where it is today. And yet, for all the advances we've made, traditional language models have remained limited in their ability to solve problems. They set out on a path, making decisions from token to token, from left to right, without ever deviating from the beaten path to explore the many other possibilities open to them.

This is where the "Tree of Thoughts" framework comes in to change things. Imagine now that the language model is standing in front of the aforementioned labyrinth. Instead of sticking to a single path, it now has the freedom to venture into every intersection, to explore every fork in the road. In this way, it can study every possible decision, weigh up the consequences of each choice and make a well-informed decision.

This framework pushes back the boundaries of the traditional language model. It doesn't just follow one path, but considers all possible paths, exploring many different lines of reasoning simultaneously. It's as if, instead of following a linear thread, the language model becomes a spider weaving a complex, multidimensional web of thoughts and decisions. In the game of 24, you have to use four digits and arithmetic operations to obtain the number 24. With the traditional model, you'd probably start by adding, subtracting, multiplying or dividing two of the numbers and continuing to operate on the result. However, with this framework, the language model can consider all possible operations simultaneously, evaluate their results, and choose the most promising one.

The "Tree of Thoughts" is not just a theoretical breakthrough. In numerous experiments, it has proved its practical effectiveness. It has improved performance in a variety of tasks requiring non-trivial searching or planning. Tasks such as creative writing or solving mini crossword puzzles have been carried out more successfully using this framework.

These models have demonstrated an increased ability to explore options, evaluate choices and make more informed decisions. They have become more effective problem-solvers, faster and more accurate than ever before.

It's a major breakthrough in the field of language models. It revolutionizes the way we solve problems, introducing a whole new way of thinking and making decisions. It opens the door to more flexible and efficient language models, capable of navigating the complex maze of problem solving with ease. This breakthrough is not only important for scientists and researchers in the field of AI, but has the potential to radically transform all fields that rely on language models for problem solving.

Context

A deep dive into language models and their use in problem solving. The constraints of current language models in terms of reasoning and decision-making. To understand the major role that language models play in our modern technology, it's essential to understand what they are and how they work. Language models are sophisticated machine learning algorithms designed to understand, interpret and generate natural language. They are the invisible cogs behind many everyday tasks, from machine translation and speech recognition to text generation and classification.

The advent of these language models has revolutionized the AI landscape, enabling them to solve problems across an incredibly wide range of tasks. However, despite their formidable power, current language models have significant limitations in terms of reasoning and decision-making. Current decision-making processes are often reduced to token-level decisions, taken from left to right during inference. This restriction implies that language models are unable to explore different paths of reasoning and make deliberate decisions. They are constrained by a linear sequence of thought, a narrow path with no possible deviation.

These limitations pose particular problems for tasks requiring complex exploration, strategic planning or major initial decision-making. Take the game of 24, in which players are faced with the arduous task of finding a combination of four numbers which, through mathematical operations, equal 24. To solve this puzzle, players must engage in an exploration of different reasoning paths and make deliberate decisions. Unfortunately, current language models find themselves stuck, unable to move freely through the maze of possibilities.

Fortunately, a solution has appeared on the horizon, in the form of a revolutionary new framework called "Tree of Thoughts". This innovative framework enables language models to explore coherent units of text, known as "thoughts", which act as intermediate steps towards problem solving. This process frees language models from their linear chains, enabling them to exercise deliberate decision-making by considering multiple paths of reasoning and evaluating the different choices available to them.

This framework is an expansion and improvement of the already popular "Chain of Thought" concept for stimulating language models. It empowers language models to consider multiple paths of reasoning, and to make more deliberate decisions by evaluating possible choices. The "Tree of Thoughts" is also particularly useful for tasks requiring exploration, strategic planning or major initial decision-making.

Using this framework, language models are able to solve problems more efficiently. They are free to explore multiple paths of reasoning and can therefore make more deliberate decisions.

Experiments were carried out to evaluate the effectiveness of the "Tree of Thoughts" framework, and the results were astounding. This framework dramatically improved the problem-solving abilities of language models. Language models who used this framework achieved superior results in solving tasks requiring non-trivial planning or searching, such as the game of 24, creative writing and mini crosswords.

Using this framework, language models can make more deliberate decisions by considering several different paths of reasoning and evaluating possible choices. This enables language models to make more informed decisions, helping them to solve problems more effectively.

The "Tree of Thoughts" framework is a significant advance in the field of language models and problem solving. This framework enables language models to explore coherent units of text and make more deliberate decisions by considering several different reasoning paths and evaluating possible choices. Experiments have shown that this framework significantly enhances the problem-solving capabilities of language models, opening up a new chapter in the field of artificial intelligence and problem-solving.

The chain of thought

This concept is based on an evolution of the popular "Chain of Thought" approach, used to stimulate language models. It enables language models to explore coherent sets of text, called "thoughts", which function as steps towards problem solving. Based on this structure, language models can then make more deliberate decisions by examining various thought paths and weighing up the available options.

This framework offers language models the opportunity to solve problems more effectively by giving them the chance to explore different paths of reasoning and make more deliberate decisions. The tree of thoughts forms the basis of the "Tree of Thoughts" framework, with each node representing a partial state of the solution. Language models can exploit this framework to explore different lines of thought and evaluate possible choices.

This framework comprises four key elements: thought decomposition, potential thought generation, heuristic state evaluation and the search algorithm. These elements are described in detail below.

Thought decomposition: The aim of this process is to divide the internal problem-solving process into coherent steps. Each step is represented by a thought, which is a coherent unit of text. Language models can use this decomposition to explore different paths of reasoning and evaluate possible options.

Generating potential thoughts: This involves generating thoughts that could be useful in solving the problem. Language models can use text generation techniques to create potential thoughts. The generated thoughts are then evaluated to determine whether they are useful for solving the problem.

Heuristic state evaluation: This phase consists of evaluating each partial state of the solution in terms of its relevance to solving the problem. Language models can use text evaluation techniques to judge each partial state. Relevant states are then used to generate potential new thoughts.

Search algorithm: This algorithm uses potential thoughts and evaluated states to explore different reasoning paths and evaluate possible choices. Language models can use search techniques to explore the thought tree and find the optimal solution.

Based on the "Tree of Thoughts" framework, language models can perform more deliberate decision-making by considering various thought paths and evaluating the available options. This enables language models to make more informed decisions and solve problems more efficiently.

Experiments conducted to evaluate the effectiveness of the framework showed that it significantly improved the problem-solving abilities of the language models. Results showed that language models using the "Tree of Thoughts" framework performed better in solving tasks requiring non-trivial planning or searching, such as the game of 24, creative writing and mini crosswords.

The framework represents a major advance in the field of language models and problem solving. It enables language models to explore coherent text units and make more deliberate decisions by considering different reasoning paths and evaluating possible options. Experiments have shown that the Tree of Thoughts framework greatly enhances the problem-solving capabilities of language models, making it a major breakthrough in the field of AI and problem-solving. Language models can use this framework to explore different avenues of thought and evaluate possible choices, enabling them to solve problems more effectively and more intentionally.

Experiences and Review of "Tree of Thoughts

In this chapter, we'll take an exciting journey through uncharted territory in the language model landscape. We'll observe a new paradigm in action, this framework (Thought Tree), standing proud and effective against its traditional counterparts. Through a series of rigorously and diligently conducted experiments, we will evaluate its performance against other problem-solving methods.

At the heart of our exploration are three challenges: the game of 24, creative writing, and mini crosswords. These tasks have been carefully chosen, not for their ease, but for their intrinsic complexity, requiring non-trivial planning and astute research. They serve as an ideal playground for our framework.

When we think of the challenge of playing 24, we imagine the cogs of the mathematical machine, turning and twisting to find the right combination of digits to reach that elusive number - 24. To meet this challenge, our language models have been fed mathematical problems, forcing them to work in a new language - that of numbers. The effectiveness of the "Tree of Thoughts" was astounding, outperforming other language models and solving problems with surprising efficiency.

Then we moved on to the creative writing challenge, asking our models to complete incomplete sentences. This challenge required not only a good understanding of grammar and syntax, but also a degree of intuition and creativity. The results were nothing short of revealing. This framework demonstrated an exceptional ability to weave complete, coherent sentences, outperforming other models with a sense of prose that seemed almost human.

Finally, we confronted our models with the complexity of mini-crosswords, training them with word definitions and assessing their ability to find matching words. Again, it proved to be an outstanding crossword solver, outperforming its competitors with almost disconcerting ease. These experiments served to confirm the executive's superiority with his ability to explore multiple lines of reasoning and make deliberate choices, solving problems more efficiently than his counterparts.

But what do these results mean for you, dear reader? Firstly, they underline the importance of flexibility and openness to new approaches. If you work with language models, think about how you can integrate elements of the "Tree of Thoughts" into your work. Secondly, they remind us that innovation is often the result of bold exploration and deep thinking. So don't be afraid to push the boundaries of your work and look for ways to improve it.

The eloquent results of the "Tree of Thoughts" framework

At the heart of all research lies evaluation, a rigorous process that separates the wheat from the chaff, reveals strengths and weaknesses, and ultimately gives meaning to our quest for knowledge. With this in mind, we have undertaken a series of experiments to demonstrate the effectiveness of the "Tree of Thoughts" framework in improving the performance of language models in problem solving.

The "Tree of Thoughts" framework, an innovative concept, stands out for its ability to explore different paths of reasoning and critically evaluate possible choices. It is not simply an incremental improvement on existing techniques, but a radical rethinking of the language model approach to problem solving.

In our experiments, we chose three distinct tasks that tested our models' abilities: the game of 24, creative writing, and mini crosswords. These tasks were specifically selected for their diversity, offering a range of demands from mathematical rigor to linguistic fluency and lexical insight.

Let's start with the game of 24. For those unfamiliar with the concept, the game involves manipulating a set of numbers through basic arithmetic operations to obtain the number 24. Our language models were trained on a dataset containing mathematical statements and evaluated in terms of their ability to solve complex mathematical statements. The effectiveness of the "Tree of Thoughts" framework was evident in the results. Compared with other language models, models using this framework performed remarkably well, solving complex mathematical statements with greater ease and accuracy.

Creative writing presented a completely different challenge. Here, the language models were fed a dataset containing incomplete sentences. Their challenge was to generate complete, coherent sentences. Again, the language models that were trained in the "Tree of Thoughts" framework demonstrated clear superiority. They created sentences that were not only complete, but also captivating and natural. It was as if the sentences had been written by a human writer, demonstrating a high degree of creativity and fluency.

Finally, we looked at mini crossword puzzles, an exercise that requires a great deal of vocabulary knowledge and the ability to decipher often cryptic clues. Language models were trained on a dataset containing word definitions, and their effectiveness was judged on their ability to correctly identify matching words. Here again, this framework proved effective. Language models trained under this regime found matching words with a speed and accuracy that outperformed other language models.

These results offer convincing evidence that the "Tree of Thoughts" framework is a powerful approach to problem solving based on language models. It promotes the exploration of multiple paths of reasoning, enabling models to make more informed and deliberate decisions. Compared with other problem-solving approaches, the framework demonstrated significant superiority in all the tasks we evaluated.

The "Tree of Thoughts" framework also offers great flexibility, making it adaptable to a variety of tasks and data types. Whether solving complex mathematical equations or generating creative sentences, this framework is up to the task. This flexibility makes the "Tree of Thoughts" framework attractive for a variety of applications, from academic research to commercial artificial intelligence.

This framework has proved to be a major advance in the field of language models and problem solving. It promotes a deeper exploration of reasoning paths and possible choices, enabling faster and more effective problem solving. The results of our experiments confirm its effectiveness and suggest that it could have a significant impact on many areas of research and application. The future of language models is exciting, and the "Tree of Thoughts" framework looks set to be a protagonist in this incredible technological adventure.

Evaluation and prospects for optimizing the framework

Our exploration is based on the "Tree of Thoughts" framework, an innovative approach aimed at optimizing the performance of language models by enabling them to follow various lines of thought and make more informed decisions. In this way, language models can solve problems more efficiently. Various experiments carried out to measure the effectiveness of this approach show that it clearly outperforms other problem-solving techniques based on language models.

In this final section, we provide a summary of the results obtained using the "Tree of Thoughts" framework, while discussing the advantages that this approach can offer for problem solving via language models. We will also discuss the promising prospects offered by this approach for future research in the fields of language models and problem solving.

Experiments conducted to evaluate the effectiveness of the "Tree of Thoughts" framework demonstrated its superiority over other problem-solving techniques based on language models. In all the tasks evaluated, language models employing the "Tree of Thoughts" framework performed significantly better than those using other approaches.

To illustrate, let's take the example of the game of 24. The language models that used the "Tree of Thoughts" framework succeeded in solving more complex mathematical statements than those that used other approaches. When it came to creative writing, the language models who used this framework succeeded in generating more coherent and natural sentences than the others. Finally, for mini crosswords, language models employing this framework found matching words faster and with greater accuracy than others.

These results attest to the effectiveness of the "Tree of Thoughts" framework for language model-based problem solving. This approach enables language models to explore different paths of reasoning and make more informed decisions, resulting in more effective problem solving. Compared with other language model-based problem-solving approaches, this framework achieved significantly better results in all the tasks evaluated.

The special feature of the framework lies in its ability to consider multiple possible reasoning paths, enabling language models to make more informed decisions and solve problems more quickly and efficiently. This method is particularly useful for tasks requiring in-depth exploration and strategic planning, as well as for tasks where initial decisions play a major role.

In addition, the "Tree of Thoughts" framework is a flexible approach that can be adapted to different tasks and different types of data. It can be used to solve a variety of problems, from complex mathematical statements to the generation of complete, coherent sentences.

The advantages of the language model-based problem-solving framework are manifold. Firstly, this approach allows language models to take into account multiple possible reasoning paths, enabling them to make more informed decisions and solve problems more quickly and efficiently. Secondly, this approach enables language models to generate more coherent and natural sentences, which is particularly important for creative writing tasks.

In addition, the "Tree of Thoughts" framework is a flexible approach that can be adapted to different tasks and different types of data. This approach can be used to solve a variety of problems, making it a versatile approach for language model-based problem solving.

As for the prospects for future research into language models and problem solving, they are very promising. The framework represents a significant advance in the field of language models and problem solving, and is likely to have a considerable impact on many areas of research and application.

Future research could focus on optimizing the "Tree of Thoughts" framework for specific tasks, as well as exploring new applications for this approach. This approach could be used to solve problems in fields such as medicine, finance and engineering.

In addition, future research could focus on exploring new language model architectures that incorporate the "Tree of Thoughts" framework. This approach could be used to improve the performance of language models in a variety of tasks, from machine translation to speech recognition.

In summary, the "Tree of Thoughts" framework is a promising approach to problem solving based on language models. This approach allows language models to consider multiple possible reasoning paths, enabling them to make more informed decisions and solve problems more quickly and efficiently. The prospects for future research into language models and problem solving are promising, and this approach is likely to have a significant impact on many areas of research and application.

-8-

Writing your first prompts

"With artificial intelligence, we have created a new form of life.... Our descendants will probably look back and say that this was the true beginning of human history."

Ben Goertzel

Artificial intelligence has revolutionized the world as we know it, changing the way we work, learn and even interact. Yet behind the veil of AI lies a key skill that is often underestimated: writing prompts. To make the most of the impressive capabilities of language models like ChatGPT, it's essential to understand the basic mechanics and best practices of writing prompts. In this introduction, we'll cover the basics of writing prompts, dive into understanding what they are, how to determine your objectives, effectively formulate your prompts, understand the importance of their length and finally, grasp the impact of their variations.

Prompts, as we saw earlier, are the triggers that prompt the language model to generate a response. While this may seem simple on the surface, the art of writing prompts is much more nuanced. Understanding how to structure a prompt, how to define your objectives and how to adjust your prompt to achieve the best possible result is a skill that can take time to master. That's the purpose of this introduction: to provide you with a solid starting point to begin this journey.

The basics of writing prompts

Writing prompts for language templates like ChatGPT can seem daunting at first. However, by understanding the fundamentals of writing prompts and adopting a structured approach, you can develop the ability to generate prompts that produce meaningful, creative and useful results. This chapter will guide you through the basics of writing prompts, to help you get started.

Understanding Prompts

A prompt is essentially an instruction for the language model. It's the input you give to the AI, telling it what you want it to do. This could be a question (e.g., "What is the capital of France?"), a writing prompt (e.g., "Write a poem about spring"), or any other task you want the AI to perform.

A key aspect to understand is that prompts are the main, and often the only, way you communicate with the AI. This means that the wording of your prompts must be clear, precise and state clearly what you want the AI to do.

Determine your Goal

Effectively formulating a prompt for a language model such as ChatGPT starts with clearly determining your objective. In other words, you need to have a clear idea of what you expect from the interaction with the AI. It may seem obvious, but a clear understanding of the desired objective is essential to obtaining useful and relevant responses.

If you're looking for a specific answer to a question, your prompt should be formulated in such a way as to direct the model to the answer you're looking for. For example, if you want to know the distance between the Earth and the Moon, your prompt might be: "What is the average distance from the Earth to the Moon?". Here, the objective is precise and the question is formulated in a straightforward way, enabling the AI to provide you with a precise answer.

If your aim is to generate creative content, such as a poem, story or joke, the wording of your prompt will be different. Here, the aim is not to get a precise factual answer, but rather to stimulate the creativity of the language model. For example, if you want the AI to write a poem about spring, your prompt might be: "Write a poem about spring that evokes feelings of rebirth and renewal". In this case, your objective is clearly defined, but leaves enough freedom for the AI to generate unique creative content.

If your aim is to obtain information on a particular subject, your prompt should be worded in such a way as to direct the AI towards the topic in question, while being open-ended enough to allow for a detailed response. For example, if you want to know more about the history of ancient Rome, your prompt might be: "Give me a detailed overview of the history of ancient Rome, starting with its foundation and ending with the fall of the Western Roman Empire". This prompt clarifies your objective and gives the AI a clear direction on what you want to know.

Formulate your Prompt

The formulation of a prompt is an important element in interaction with a language model such as GPT-4. A prompt is essentially an instruction or request addressed to the model, guiding it on the nature of the text to be generated. However, it's important to note that AI doesn't understand context or intent in the same way as a human being. It can only rely on the information you give it to generate a response. This means that the clarity and precision of your prompt is crucial to obtaining the desired response.

When writing your prompt, consider incorporating these aspects:

1. Subject specificity

If you want the AI to write a text on a certain subject, you need to be as specific as possible in your request. For example, instead of asking the AI to "Write an article on history", a more precise instruction might be "Write a 500-word article on the French Revolution, focusing on the causes and consequences of the event."

2. Style and tone

It's also useful to indicate the style or tone you'd like the generated text to have. For example, do you want an academic, informal, humorous, serious or romantic tone? To get a rhyming poem, for example, you could ask "Write a rhyming poem about the beauty of autumn."

3. Text length

Another aspect to specify is the length of the text you want. Language templates are capable of generating texts of various lengths, from one-sentence tweets to multi-paragraph blog posts. So specify whether you want a short summary or a detailed analysis.

For example, "Give me a two-paragraph summary of Fyodor Dostoevsky's 'Crime and Punishment'." or "Write a detailed analysis of 'Crime and Punishment', focusing on the theme of guilt."

Bear in mind that, although precise and detailed prompt formulation can greatly improve the quality of the AI's response, language models have inherent limitations and won't always produce perfect results. Their performance depends largely on the quality and quantity of the training data on which they have been trained.

Prompt length

When it comes to creating a prompt for an AI-based language model, such as GPT-4, the length of the prompt plays an important role in getting the desired response. There is no universal ideal length for a prompt, as it largely depends on the nature of the question or task you're asking the model to perform.

For certain types of task, a short, precise prompt may be sufficient. For example, if you want to know the capital of France, a simple "What is the capital of France?" will suffice. In this case, a longer prompt could even be counter-productive, as it could dilute the main request or introduce superfluous elements that could confuse the AI.

However, in other situations, longer, more detailed prompts can be beneficial. For example, if you want the AI to write an article on a complex topic or answer a question requiring in-depth analysis, a more detailed prompt can help guide the response. You could provide details on style, tone, intended audience or specific points to cover in the response.

It's also important to bear in mind that AI-based language models have a limit to the number of tokens they can process at any one time. A "token" is a unit of text, which can be a word, character or punctuation. For example, the GPT-4 model can process up to 4096 tokens at a time. This limit includes both prompt and generated response tokens.

Therefore, if your prompt is extremely long, this may limit the amount of text the AI can generate in response. If a very long prompt is required, it may be preferable to divide it into several shorter prompts, allowing the AI to generate a response to each part before moving on to the next. The key is to formulate your prompts in such a way as to achieve the desired results. This may require some trial and error, as well as a thorough understanding of how the specific language model you're using interprets and responds to prompts. The aim is to find the right balance between accuracy, clarity and length of the prompt to maximize the quality of the response generated by the AI.

Prompts Variations

In the fascinating and complex world of artificial intelligence, the principle of prompt variation plays a significant role. This variation, which may appear minimal on the surface, has the potential to significantly influence the responses generated by a language model. Prompt variation thus offers a rich field of experimentation for refining interaction with AI and steering the conversation in a more productive direction.

Prompt variation can relate to different aspects of the prompt: the wording of the question, the level of detail, the tone or style, and even the presupposition implicit in the prompt. Each of these variations can lead to different responses from the AI, depending on how it interprets and processes the prompt.

Formulating the question

The way in which a question is posed can significantly influence the AI's response. For example, the question "What is democracy?" is a direct request for information, while "Can you explain the concept of democracy?" invites the AI to adopt a more didactic approach. Both prompts address the same subject, but the slight variation in wording can lead to different answers, better matching the user's expectations in each case.

Detail level

The level of detail in a prompt is also decisive. A vague or general prompt can lead to an equally vague response, whereas a more precise and detailed prompt can help steer the AI towards a more relevant answer. For example, "Tell me a story" is a fairly general prompt that leaves a lot to the AI's interpretation. On the other hand, "Tell me an adventure story set in the Middle Ages" gives the AI a more precise framework for generating the text, which can lead to a response more suited to the user's expectations.

Tone and Style

The tone or style of the prompt can also influence the AI's response. For example, a prompt given in a humorous tone, such as "What would be the worst job for a robot?" may invite the AI to adopt a humorous tone in its response. Similarly, a formal or academic prompt may lead the AI to produce a response that matches this tone.

Presuppositions

Finally, the presuppositions implicit in a prompt can also affect the AI's response. For example, asking the AI "What is your opinion of X?" presupposes that the AI has opinions, which it does not. Such wording can lead to confused or misleading answers. In contrast, a prompt like "What are the arguments for and against X?" invites the AI to provide a more objective, factual analysis.

In short, mastering the art of prompt variation can greatly enrich interactions with AI. As with any skill, this requires practice and experimentation. Over time, you'll discover the subtle nuances that can make all the difference in the way the AI understands and responds to your prompts.

These basic principles should help you get started writing prompts for AI language templates. As you gain experience, you'll discover new techniques and strategies that will enable you to improve your prompter writing skills even further.

Common types of prompts

Prompts are incredibly versatile tools for interacting with AI language models. Their use can vary considerably depending on the desired goal. Let's take a look at some of the common types of prompt use.

Quick information

One of the most common uses of prompts is to request information from the AI. For example, the AI might be asked to provide a detailed summary of a specific topic, such as "Explain the history of the American Civil War" or "What is photosynthesis?". This type of prompt is usually quite direct and specific, and the AI will respond by providing as much information as possible on the topic in question. These prompts are particularly useful for users seeking detailed information on a specific topic.

Creative speed

Prompts can also be used to generate creative content. For example, the AI could be asked to write a short story based on a certain set of parameters, such as "Write a science fiction story where an astronaut encounters a friendly alien life form". Creative prompts can also be used to generate poems, movie dialogue, jokes, and many other types of content. The open-ended nature of these prompts gives the AI plenty of freedom to generate unique and interesting responses.

Advice

The field of Artificial Intelligence has come a long way since its beginnings, evolving from simple recommendation systems to highly sophisticated language models capable of providing practical advice on a wide range of topics. These systems, when properly prompted by "advice prompts", can become invaluable tools for users seeking suggestions or recommendations.

An advice prompt is a request for information or guidance made by the user. These can be simple questions, such as "What are the best books to read to understand personal finance?" or "Give me ideas for outdoor activities to do during the summer". In response to these prompts, the AI will generate suggestions based on the information available in its training system.

One of the key advantages of advice prompts is their flexibility. They can cover almost any area of interest, from learning a new skill to planning a trip, and can be tailored to suit different levels of specificity. For example, a prompt can be general, such as "What are the basics of investing?", or specific, such as "What are the advantages and disadvantages of index funds versus individual stocks?".

However, it is important to note that advice prompts are not a substitute for human expert advice. The suggestions generated by the AI are based on the information available during its training, and they may not take into account recent changes in a particular field or the specific nuances of an individual's situation. For these reasons, advice prompts should be used as a starting point or source of inspiration, rather than as a substitute for professional advice.

Finally, it's also important to be aware of the importance of correctly formulating advice prompts. A well-crafted prompt is specific, clear and avoids ambiguity. For example, instead of asking "What should I do?", a user might ask "What steps should I take to start an e-commerce business?". A well-formulated prompt helps the AI to provide a more precise and useful answer.

In short, advice prompts are a valuable tool in AI interaction, allowing users to tap into a vast knowledge base for suggestions and advice on a multitude of topics. Used judiciously, they can enrich our understanding, stimulate our creativity and help us make informed decisions.

Simulation Prompts

Simulation prompts offer an interesting and effective way of engaging with artificial intelligence. By asking the AI to simulate a certain situation or role, we can explore a variety of scenarios and interactions that might otherwise be difficult to realize. This approach can be both playful and practical, offering opportunities for learning, exploration and personal development.

Simulation of professional roles

One of the most common applications of simulation prompts is to ask the AI to play the role of an expert in a certain field. For example, we might ask the AI to simulate a conversation with a historian. In this case, the prompt might be something like "Can you explain to me the cause of the First World War as if you were a historian?" In response, the AI would use its vast knowledge bases to generate an answer that resembles what a historian might give.

Similarly, we could ask the AI to play the role of a life coach. In this case, the prompt might be "As a life coach, what would you advise me to do to manage my stress at work?" Here, the AI could provide advice based on general knowledge of psychology and stress management.

Simulation of fictional characters

Simulation prompts can also be used to ask AI to play the role of fictional characters. This can be a fun way to create interactive stories or play role-playing games. For example, the AI could be asked to simulate a conversation with Harry Potter, asking "If you were Harry Potter, how would you describe your first year at Hogwarts?"

Simulation of hypothetical situations

Finally, simulation prompts can also be used to explore hypothetical situations. For example, the AI could be asked to simulate a conversation between two characters in a futuristic scenario, by asking "Imagine a conversation between a human engineer and an advanced artificial intelligence in space in 2200".

Overall, simulation prompts offer a variety of opportunities for interesting interactions with artificial intelligence. Whether we're looking to learn, explore, create, or simply have fun, these prompts can help make our interactions with AI more engaging and rewarding.

Ready for analysis

Analysis prompts play a major role in exploiting advanced AI capabilities. They enable us to solicit a response based on a systematic evaluation of the information, asking the AI to go beyond simply providing information or generating creative content. These prompts aim for a deeper interpretation or evaluation.

Let's take the example "Analyze real estate market trends over the last ten years". This prompt requires an understanding of the notion of real estate market trends and access to an up-to-date database to examine these trends over a decade. This is a challenge for AI, as it must not only access accurate data, but also analyze it in a meaningful way to deduce relevant trends.

However, at present, it should be noted that language models such as GPT-4 are not able to consult real-time information or access specific databases for updates. They are trained on a large corpus of pre-existing texts up to a certain point in time (for example, GPT-4 was trained on texts available up to September 2021). Consequently, their analysis would be based on the data available at that time.

In the case of the second example, "What are the main themes of George Orwell's novel '1984'?", the AI is better placed to give a precise answer. This is due to the static nature of the literary text, which doesn't change over time like real estate market trends. Based on the textual data on which it has been trained, GPT-4 could provide an informed analysis of the novel's key themes, such as state surveillance, individual freedom, truth and manipulation.

However, it's important to note that, despite AI's impressive advances, it can't replace human analysis, particularly in areas that require critical thinking, subjective interpretation or aesthetic appreciation. Analysis prompts serve as a starting point for more complex and nuanced questions, and they demonstrate how far language models have progressed in terms of understanding natural language. However, they also highlight the current limitations of these models, and the areas where human interaction and reflection remain indispensable.

These types of prompts are just a few examples of how prompts can be used to interact with AI. Depending on your specific needs and objectives, you can use these types of prompts as a starting point and adapt them to achieve the desired results. The important thing is to be clear and specific in your prompt, and to give the AI as much detail and context as possible to help it provide the best possible response.

Step-by-step prompts

Creating a prompt for a language model like ChatGPT is both an art and a science. You need to master the right balance between technique and creativity to get the most out of these powerful tools. The process of writing a prompt involves not only an understanding of how the model works - and we've just seen the basics - but also an ability to formulate clear, precise questions and statements that will effectively guide the model towards the kind of response you're looking for. So, how do you achieve this balance and generate prompts that will produce the results you're looking for?

The first thing to understand when writing prompts for a language model is that these systems are not omniscient. They don't have access to real-time information and can't grasp the context or intent of a request without it being explicitly presented in the prompt. It's up to us, as users, to provide the necessary context and clarity. The ability of these templates to generate coherent, creative and informative texts is astounding. They can write articles, compose poetry, answer factual questions, simulate conversations and much more.

Creating an effective prompt is therefore a process of adaptation and adjustment, involving understanding the model's capabilities and limitations, formulating clear and precise questions, and adjusting these questions as necessary to achieve the desired results. By understanding the model's basic structure and refining our approach, we can learn to work with the model more effectively and productively.

So how do you go about writing an effective prompt? Let's look at a step-by-step approach that will help you understand how to write a prompt, evaluate its effectiveness and adjust it as necessary to achieve the best possible results.

Step 1: Define the objective

The first step in prompt engineering is to define precisely the objective of your interaction with the model. This objective will be the starting point for formulating your prompt, and will guide the type of response you expect from the language model. The importance of clearly defining your objective before you start interacting with the model cannot be overstated, as this is what will steer the language model in the right direction.

To illustrate this point, let's take an example. Let's say you're working on a project to write a science fiction novel, and you're looking for AI help in developing a complex scenario involving time travel. Your objective could then be formulated as follows: "Generate a detailed and coherent scenario for a science fiction novel featuring time travel".

This objective is both specific and precise. It makes it clear to the model that you're looking to generate a detailed screenplay (not just an idea or synopsis), that the screenplay must be coherent (i.e. logically consistent and consistent) and that it must concern a science fiction novel with time travel (which provides a genre framework and a central element of the screenplay).

With this objective clearly defined, you can then formulate an appropriate prompt for the template. For example, you might start with "Create a detailed and coherent scenario for a science fiction novel that involves time travel". This prompt is directly aligned with your objective and gives the model a clear direction for generating the answer.

By defining your objective clearly and precisely from the outset, you can increase the chances of getting a useful and relevant response from the language model. Don't underestimate the time-saving benefits of taking the time from the outset to define your objective in detail. It's important to validate this first step in the prompt engineering process.

Step 2: Understanding the model

Understanding how the language model works is an essential step in interacting effectively with AI. Models like ChatGPT and those previously mentioned, based on a "Transformer" architecture, are trained on a vast amount of text and generate responses by predicting the most likely sequence of words. It's a statistical process based on probabilities, not deep contextual understanding or real-world knowledge. This is a far cry from the kind of global AI awareness we might fear if we were to rely solely on a James Cameron-style scenario.

For example, if we give ChatGPT the prompt "The sky is usually...", the model scours its internal database, analyzing billions of sentences to determine which word or phrase is statistically most likely to end that sentence. In this case, it might generate "blue" as the answer, because, according to the data on which it was trained, "The sky is usually blue" is a common phrase in human speech.

It's important to note that the model doesn't "know" that the sky is blue because of a scientific understanding of atmospheric phenomena. It produces this response because it has been trained on texts that frequently use this phrase. In other words, its "knowledge" is actually a statistical modeling of trends in the text data on which it has been trained. From this we can easily deduce that the term "intelligence" is, to say the least, overused in today's language models.

This also means that language models are limited by the data on which they have been trained. This is why GAFAM (Google, Apple, Facebook, Amazon, and Microsoft) among others spend billions of dollars on training data for their models. Because if a concept, event or idea wasn't present in the model's training data, the model will struggle to generate accurate information about it. For example, ChatGPT can't provide real-time updates on world events, because it can't access the Internet or real-time information sources. It can only generate answers from the information contained in the data it was trained on dating back to 2021.

What's more, language models don't have consciousness or feelings. When ChatGPT generates a response, it doesn't "think" or "feel" anything. It simply performs a statistical calculation to determine the most likely response to a given prompt. It's important to realize that ChatGPT and its competitors react like a calculator displaying the answer; there's no affect behind it, or it's been simulated. Understanding these aspects of how language models work can help you ask questions and provide prompts more effectively, taking into account the strengths and limitations of these models.

Step 3: Writing the prompt

Once you've defined your objective and analyzed your audience, you can move on to the third step: writing the prompt. This step requires particular attention, as it's the starting point for the interaction between the user and the AI model. The prompt you formulate must be carefully designed to guide the AI towards the type of response you expect. You'll need a lot of practice, too, to fully grasp the subtleties. I've included a practice section at the end of the book so that you can practice and gain competence with practice.

Write for a detailed response :

If your aim is to get a detailed, in-depth answer, your prompt should be worded in such a way as to explicitly ask for such an answer. For example, instead of asking "What is photosynthesis?", which might result in a simple, straightforward answer, you could ask "Could you explain the process of photosynthesis in detail?". By using this prompt, you clearly signal to the model that you expect a more complex and detailed answer. You could also add to this example "Could you explain in detail the process of photosynthesis to an 8-year-old child and give some examples?", then you'll understand the incredible power and usefulness of these conversational models if you have children. But this also applies to anyone who wants to discover or learn a new subject more easily.

Writing for a specific style or tone :

If you want the template to generate text in a specific style or tone, it's essential to state this explicitly in the prompt. For example, if you want the template to write a story in the style of Ernest Hemingway, you could phrase your prompt as follows: "Write a short adventure story in the style of Ernest Hemingway". By indicating the desired style directly in the prompt, you give the model a clear direction for generating the text.

You can also ask the model to write as if he or she were a certain person or character. For example, you could ask "How would Harry Potter describe his first year at Hogwarts?". Here, you invite the model to adopt Harry Potter's point of view and narrative style, which can lead to an interesting and creative response.

It's important to remember that, while these techniques can help to achieve the desired type of response, they don't guarantee a perfect result. Transformer-based language models are powerful, but they have their limits and can sometimes produce unexpected or inconsistent responses. That's why continuous experimentation and fine-tuning are essential to mastering the art of prompt engineering.

Step 4: Response evaluation

It's very important to evaluate the response generated by the AI once you've received it. This allows you to check whether the response provided has achieved the objective set when the prompt was formulated. This evaluation generally consists of checking whether the response meets your initial objective, or whether it has generated the type of text you had in mind when writing the prompt.

Take, for example, the case where you ask the AI to "Write a poem about the sunset". A satisfactory response might be a poem that describes the sunset in a lyrical way, uses poetic metaphors, and perhaps even evokes feelings or impressions.

However, if the AI generates a factual description of the sunset process without using poetic language, you may find that the answer hasn't achieved your goal. In other words, even if the answer is correct and informative, it has failed to produce the specific type of text you were looking for.

If you're not satisfied, you should consider reformulating your prompt. In our example, a reformulation might be "Write a lyrical poem that evokes the feelings associated with a sunset". By adding specific details about the type of poetry and emotional tone, you further guide the AI towards producing the desired response.

This evaluation stage is essential for refining your interaction with the AI. By learning from each response and adjusting your prompts accordingly, you can gradually improve the quality of the responses generated by the AI, and achieve more accurate and relevant results. Numerous iterations can then be carried out until the desired perfect result is achieved - and this is perfectly normal with this method.

Step 5: Iteration and refinement

The art of writing prompts is not an exact science, and even the most experienced designers can't always predict how a language model will respond to a specific request. That's where iteration and refinement come in - two key processes that can help turn a mediocre interaction with a language model into an accurate and informative one.

To illustrate this process, let me give you an example. Let's say you ask ChatGPT (I'm using the best-known one as an example, but this applies to all other models) to "Tell a science fiction story". This is a pretty broad prompt, and the model can respond with a variety of scenarios. Let's say that in its response, the template creates a story about an advanced civilization on Mars, but you were actually interested in a time travel story.

This is where the iteration and refinement stage comes in. Based on the initial response, you can rephrase your prompt to make it more specific, making it clear that you want a time travel story. So you might try a prompt like "Tell a science fiction story about time travel".

In this second attempt, the model is much more likely to generate the story you had in mind. However, let's assume that in its response, the model emphasizes complex technical aspects of time travel, when you actually wanted a more character-driven story. Again, you can refine your prompt further, for example by asking "Tell a science fiction story about time travel, centered on the characters and their experiences".

Each iteration brings you closer to the story you had in mind. It may take several rounds of fine-tuning, but the iteration process is essential to maximize the accuracy and usefulness of the language model's response.

As I mentioned earlier, this is normal and don't be discouraged if you don't get exactly what you want on the first interaction. Use every response as an opportunity to learn and refine your prompt. By refining your queries and clarifying your expectations, you can guide the template towards generating content that best meets your needs. Don't forget to write them down or save them for future use!

Step 6: Documentation and sharing

When you get a response that meets your objectives, document your prompt and the answer you got. This is a good practice, especially if you work in a team or plan to use similar prompts in the future, as it will be a really valuable aid (note-taking is important). What's more, share your successes and failures with the community of users of the template you're using, as this can help others to learn and improve their own prompt writing skills. You too can learn from their mistakes and the successful prompts they share with you.

As you can see, writing prompts is a process that requires strategic thinking, an understanding of language patterns, a certain amount of creativity and a lot of iteration. But with practice, you can become increasingly proficient and effective at creating prompts that get the results you want.

The art of writing prompts for language models, such as ChatGPT, is a skill that can be honed with time and practice. Each step in the process, from defining the objective to evaluating the response, understanding the model and writing the prompt, plays a decisive role in achieving the desired results. It's important to remember that these models, while incredibly sophisticated, are not omniscient and depend heavily on the quality and clarity of the prompt to generate appropriate responses.

Iteration and refinement are essential aspects of this process. It's rare to get it right the first time, and every attempt is an opportunity to learn and improve your prompt writing skills. Documenting and sharing your experiences, both successes and failures, are also beneficial practices that can help improve not only your own skill, but that of the community as a whole. There's a real spirit of collaboration and mutual aid in the use of this new technology among users, with the discovery of new fields of possibility that we'd never have thought of on our own. You can find support groups on Facebook, for example, or on Reddit if you want to expand your possibilities.

-9-

Mastering the specifics of order prompts

"Artificial intelligence is just a reflection of us. It will not surpass us. It will become us."

Max Tegmark

The importance of specificity

Specificity is a key concept for understanding and mastering the art of prompts when interacting with an AI language model like ChatGPT. It's about providing clear, precise and detailed instructions to guide the model towards the desired response. It's a delicate balance between giving enough information to direct the model, while leaving enough room for innovation and creativity.

When we talk about specificity in the context of prompts, we're referring to two main dimensions: specificity of subject and specificity of form.

The specificity of the subject

When it comes to topic specificity, we're referring to how clearly you tell the template what topic you want it to cover. For example, instead of simply asking ChatGPT to "write an essay on history", you could make your prompt more specific by asking "write a 1000-word essay on the impact of World War II on the global economy". By clearly indicating the subject of the essay, you direct the model to the precise area you want it to focus on, increasing the chances of getting a relevant and informative response. The more "Parameters" you give it (1000 words, World War II, global economy) in your specifics the more relevant your result will be.

The specificity of form

Form specificity refers to the way you want the template to structure and present its response. For example, ask yourself whether you want the answer to be in the form of a paragraph, a list, a poem, a dialogue, and so on. Form specificity can also involve the desired length of the response, tone (formal, informal, humorous, serious, etc.) and other stylistic elements.

To repeat the example, instead of simply asking "Explain Cosmology to me", you could make your prompt more specific by asking "Explain the history of Cosmology to me as if you were writing a rhyming children's book". This gives the model a clear indication not only of the topic, but also of how you want the information presented.

Specificity in practice

Applying specificity when writing prompts can take a little practice and experimentation. It can be helpful to start with more general prompts, then gradually refine your approach by adding more detail and precision. It's also important to bear in mind that over-specification can sometimes be counter-productive, as it can limit the model's ability to generate creative and innovative responses.

It's worth noting that even with the right specification, the model may not always generate the exact answer you're hoping for. This is where iteration comes in, a major aspect of prompt engineering. If a prompt doesn't produce the desired results, it may be worth reviewing and adjusting your level of specificity.

In short, specificity plays an important role in getting accurate and relevant responses from ChatGPT. By mastering topic and form specificity, you can effectively guide the model to produce the results you're looking for. However, it's important to remember that balance is key, and that iteration is an essential aspect of the process.

Directing AI towards desired results

The starting point for any interaction with a language model is the prompt. The prompt is the initial impulse that directs the model and helps it understand what you want it to do. It's essential to understand that the model knows nothing about your intentions until it sees the prompt. It has no context other than what is directly provided in the prompt and any learning data it has received during training. This means that the clarity and precision of your prompt are essential to guide the AI towards the results you want.

Good prompts are generally specific, directive and explicit in their instructions. For example, if you want the model to write an argumentative essay on global warming, a good prompt might be "Write a 500-word argumentative essay on the causes and consequences of global warming, with an introduction, three main paragraphs and a conclusion." This prompt gives the model a clear structure to follow and precise guidelines on the content to include.

It can also be useful to include in your prompt indications of the style or tone you want. For example, if you want a formal essay, you could add "use a formal academic style" to your prompt. Or if you want a more humorous or light-hearted response, you might say "write this in a humorous, light-hearted tone". Language models are probabilistic systems that generate responses based on patterns they've learned in training. Sometimes, they may interpret your prompt in a way you hadn't intended, or they may simply generate a response that isn't quite what you'd hoped for.

When this happens - and it's bound to happen sooner or later - don't be discouraged. Think of it as an opportunity to refine your prompt and learn more about how the model interprets instructions. Sometimes, a slight rewording of your prompt or the addition of a few extra details can make all the difference.

Finally, don't forget that patience and perseverance are essential when it comes to working with language models. With time and experience, you'll learn to write prompts that effectively direct AI towards the results you want, opening up a world of possibilities for using these incredibly powerful technologies.

Case studies of very specific prompts

In the complex field of conversational artificial intelligence, the way in which we ask a question or, in AI terms, formulate a "prompt", can considerably influence the relevance and accuracy of the response obtained. The more specific and descriptive the prompt, the better the AI is able to identify the intention behind the request, and thus produce an answer that fully satisfies our expectations.

The specificity of a prompt is like a compass for the AI model. It guides it through the vast amount of information it has learned, and enables it to target its responses more precisely. In other words, a well-constructed, detailed prompt can make the difference between a vague, generic response and a precise, useful one.

Yet knowing how to formulate effective prompts can be confusing. How much detail is needed? How can we convey our intent clearly without restricting the AI's creativity? To answer these questions, we'll look at a set of revealing case studies. These examples demonstrate how users have succeeded in formulating very specific prompts, leading to impressive results that not only met their initial expectations, but sometimes even exceeded them.

In this section, we'll dive into an in-depth exploration of these case studies, with the aim of learning valuable lessons and understanding how we can all better interact with AI models to get the answers we need. Through these concrete examples, we'll demonstrate the power of precision in prompt formulation and the significant impact it can have on the effectiveness of our interactions with AI.

Case study 1: A storytelling challenge

In this case study, a user engaged in interaction with an AI like ChatGPT with the specific aim of generating a unique and engaging science fiction story. This is no simple task - such a story requires a captivating setting, a solid plot, interesting characters and meaningful themes. How to guide the language model to achieve this result? The user opted for a strategic prompt engineering approach.

Instead of simply asking ChatGPT to create a "science fiction story", the user specified key details about what he wanted from the story. He asked for a story that "takes place in the distant future, with robots, spaceships, and a plot revolving around a mysterious artifact". By specifying these elements, the user gave the model a solid base on which to build the story.

This detailed initial prompt enabled ChatGPT to generate a story that closely aligned with the user's expectations. The resulting story took place in the desired futuristic setting, incorporated robots and spaceships as key elements, and revolved around the mysterious artifact as a central plot pivot.

However, it is important to note that the quality of the story was not only due to the specificity of the initial prompt. The user also interacted with ChatGPT iteratively throughout the generation of the story. For example, if the model drifted towards an unwanted sub-theme or plot element, the user reformulated or adjusted the prompt to bring the story back on track.

This case study illustrates the importance of a detailed and specific prompt when generating complex texts, as well as the essential role of continuous interaction and iteration in achieving the desired result. It highlights the creative potential of language models like ChatGPT when guided by a strategic combination of specificity, clarity and continuous user participation.

Case study 2: Interview simulation

For this user, ChatGPT proved to be an invaluable tool for preparing job interviews. The candidate was seeking a position as a software engineer in a start-up focused on artificial intelligence. This is a specific role, with unique challenges and skills, requiring targeted and detailed interview preparation.

Rather than simply asking ChatGPT to provide "job interview questions", which could have resulted in a wide range of generic questions, the user specified his request. He used the prompt: "Provide interview questions specific to a software engineer role in an AI-focused start-up". This guided the model to generate relevant questions that precisely matched the type of interview the candidate was expecting.

For example, the model generated questions such as "How would you balance the need for rapid iteration with maintaining code quality in a growth-stage start-up?", "What are the most important ethical considerations when building AI systems for real-time use?" or "How did you overcome a particular technical challenge in a recent AI project?". These questions enabled the candidate to reflect on and prepare for the kinds of specific, nuanced questions he might encounter in his interview.

In addition, the candidate also used ChatGPT to simulate answers to these questions, creating a kind of "role play" with the model. By providing answers to these questions and asking for feedback or follow-up questions, the candidate was able to refine his answers and prepare even better for the upcoming interview.

This use case illustrates perfectly how prompt engineering can be used to transform a generic interaction with a language model into a personalized and highly useful experience. By being precise in the formulation of his prompts, the user was able to harness ChatGPT's potential to create a realistic and relevant job interview simulation.

Case study 3: Designing a marketing campaign

In this third case study, we explore the application of AI, and more specifically the ChatGPT language model, in the field of marketing. A user wanted to harness the power of artificial intelligence to create an innovative marketing campaign for a new eco-friendly clothing brand.

Instead of simply asking the AI to provide "ideas for a marketing campaign", the user gave more details about the product, brand and values they wanted to highlight. This level of specificity is important when working with language models like ChatGPT, as it gives them context to generate more precise and relevant responses.

In detail, the user phrased his prompt as follows: "Generate ideas for a marketing campaign for 'Green Threads', a new eco-friendly clothing brand that values sustainability, innovation and inclusivity". By providing this context, the user directed ChatGPT to the precise type of campaign they wanted to develop.

In response, ChatGPT was able to draw on this information to propose campaign ideas that were not only creative, but also directly aligned with the brand's identity and values. For example, the AI suggested the organization of a live virtual fashion show where models wear 'Green Threads' creations in natural settings, highlighting the connection between eco-responsible clothing and nature. In addition, AI proposed the idea of a social networking campaign centered on the story of everyday "green heroes" - ordinary people who make extraordinary efforts to live sustainably.

Overall, this case demonstrates the effectiveness of prompt engineering in generating creative, customized solutions. By providing precise and relevant details in the prompt, the user was able to obtain campaign ideas that were directly aligned with the brand's values and objectives, maximizing the effectiveness and relevance of the marketing campaign.

Case study 4: Writing a speech

In this fourth case, we examine a slightly different application of text generation, where the user has enlisted ChatGPT's help to write a graduation speech. The challenge here is twofold: not only must the model produce a text that respects the conventions of a formal speech, but it must also adapt to the user's specific voice and the message he wishes to convey.

Initially, the user could have chosen to simply ask ChatGPT to "write a graduation speech". However, such a general prompt could produce a variety of results, as "a graduation speech" could mean many different things. It could be a speech given by a student, or by a member of university staff, or even by a celebrity guest. What's more, the speech could cover a range of topics, from personal memories of university life to advice for the future.

To obtain a more precise and useful response, the user chose to be more specific in his prompt. He indicated that he was the rector of the university, which helped frame the tone and content of the speech. He also indicated that the speech should be inspirational, which gave the model an indication of the emotional tone to adopt. Finally, he specified that the speech should focus on the challenges and opportunities of the post-pandemic era, which helped guide the model on the speech's central theme.

The result of this more detailed and specific approach was a speech that not only respected the appropriate formal conventions, but was also customized for the user's role, desired tone and the specific message they wanted to convey. This example illustrates the power of specificity and adaptation in writing prompts. The aim is not to constrain the template's creativity, but rather to give it a clear direction that will enable it to generate content that effectively addresses the user's specific needs.

This case study highlights the importance of being both precise and descriptive in your prompts. By guiding the AI with relevant details and clear direction, you can get answers that are not only relevant, but also customized to meet your specific needs. It's a process that may require a little more thought and effort at first, but the results can be incredibly rewarding.

These case studies illustrate the power of specificity in prompts. By being more specific and descriptive in your prompts, you can guide the AI more effectively and get answers that are more relevant and useful to your specific needs.

-10-

Advanced incentive techniques

"Artificial intelligence is a tool, not a threat."

Rodney Brooks

Interacting with AI-based language models like ChatGPT can be compared to navigating across a vast, unexplored ocean. Every conversation is a journey, and to navigate effectively, it's necessary to understand how to steer the trajectory of the conversation towards the desired destination. This is where two essential skills come into play: sequencing and adding progressive details.

We're going to immerse ourselves in these valuable techniques that will enable you to optimize your interactions with AI language models. We'll explore how sequencing and adding progressive detail can not only improve the accuracy of AI-generated responses, but also give you greater control over the flow of the conversation.

Progressive sequences and details

As you become more familiar with prompt design, you'll discover the importance of sequencing and adding progressive detail. This chapter will explore how these techniques can enrich your interactions with AI language models, lead to more precise and detailed responses, and help you better control the flow of conversation.

Understanding scheduling

Scheduling is the technique of asking questions or giving instructions in an orderly and logical way. It is particularly useful when you need to ask several related questions, or ask the AI to process a task in several stages. If you want the AI to write an article on the history of artificial intelligence, you could start by asking it to list the main stages in that history. Then you can ask specific questions about each stage, asking for more detail or asking the AI to highlight key points or implications of each stage.

This sequential approach helps to structure the conversation and guide the AI through the task in a more controlled way. This can improve the accuracy of the AI's response and make it easier to get the information you're looking for.

Add progressive details

Adding progressive details is another key technique. Instead of giving all the necessary information in a single prompt, you can introduce it gradually, as the conversation progresses.

This technique is particularly useful for more complex tasks or longer conversations. For example, if you want the AI to create a story, you could start by defining the basic framework, then introduce the characters, establish the plot, and so on. By introducing these elements one at a time, you can guide the AI through the process of creating the story and have more control over the end result.

Progressive scheduling and detailing in action

Let's take a concrete example. Let's say you want AI to help you plan a trip. Instead of immediately asking "Plan a two-week trip to Europe", you could start by asking more general questions, such as "What are the must-visit countries in Europe?". Once you've got a list of countries, you can then ask more specific questions about each country, such as "What are the main tourist sites in France?" or "What's the best time of year to visit Germany?". Finally, once you've gathered all this information, you can ask the AI to help you create a detailed itinerary.

By using scheduling and progressive detailing, you can turn a complex task into a series of simpler, more manageable tasks. This can make the process more enjoyable for you and improve the quality of the results you get from AI.

Scheduling and progressive detail are powerful tools in your prompter arsenal. However, they require some practice to master. As always, don't hesitate to experiment with these techniques and learn from your mistakes. Over time, you'll become increasingly comfortable with these concepts and be able to use them effectively to get the most out of your interactions with AI language models.

Implicit and explicit instructions

The creation of an effective prompt goes beyond the elaboration of a simple question or a direct command. This is where implicit and explicit instructions come into play. Understanding the difference between these two types of instructions, and knowing when to use them, can help you hone your skills as a prompt engineer and maximize the effectiveness of your prompts.

Explicit instructions

The use of explicit text generation instructions is an effective way of communicating clear, language model-specific expectations. These instructions provide precise guidelines on the content, tone, format and even length of the expected response. They act as a kind of "roadmap", guiding the language model in producing responses that are specifically tailored to the user's needs.

Take, for example, the following request to ChatGPT: "Write a 300-word summary of George Orwell's novel '1984'". Here, the user gives explicit instructions that define both the content and the length of the response. The content should be a summary of the novel '1984', and the length should be around 300 words. These instructions help the language model to understand precisely what the user expects.

Explicit instructions are particularly useful when the user has a clear idea of what he or she wants. For example, if a student asks ChatGPT to "Write a two-page argumentative essay on the effects of climate change on agriculture", the explicit instruction provides clear guidance on the type of text (an argumentative essay), the topic (the effects of climate change on agriculture) and the length (two pages).

Another example might be a business request, such as "Write a formal follow-up e-mail after a sales meeting, highlighting the key points discussed and proposing a next step". Here, the explicit instruction indicates not only the format (a formal follow-up e-mail), but also the specific content to be included (key points discussed, a proposed next step).

However, the use of explicit instructions can sometimes restrict the creativity of the language model. For example, if you ask ChatGPT to "Tell a 500-word story about a trip to the mountains", you're giving it a specific length and a specific topic. This can limit the model's ability to elaborate on details or take unexpected story turns. That's why, while explicit instructions are useful for focusing results, it can also be beneficial to leave some room for creativity and exploration.

Implicit instructions

Implicit instructions are a major aspect of interaction with language models like ChatGPT. Unlike explicit instructions, which clearly detail what you expect as a response, implicit instructions are more subtle. They are less direct, offering greater latitude for the response generated by the model. Implicit instructions are formulated to suggest rather than prescribe the direction the response should take.

Let's take the example of the question "What do you think of George Orwell's '1984'?" In this case, you're asking ChatGPT an open-ended question. You're not explicitly asking for a summary of the book, or a literary analysis, or a review. Instead, you give ChatGPT leeway to interpret your request and formulate an answer that can take many forms.

In such a situation, ChatGPT might choose to share a thematic analysis of the work, explore the book's cultural impact, or perhaps discuss why '1984' is considered a literary classic. The model could also offer a perspective on the parallels between the book's themes and contemporary society. So, by using an implicit instruction, you get a variety of possible answers, all of which could answer your question.

The advantage of implicit instructions is that they allow greater exploration of a subject and can often lead to more creative or unexpected answers. For example, if you ask ChatGPT "What makes a story interesting?", you don't specify whether you want a literary, psychological, or cultural perspective. This gives ChatGPT the freedom to explore various dimensions of the question, all of which could offer useful insights.

However, it's important to note that using implicit instructions can also lead to answers that aren't exactly what you had in mind. For example, if you ask ChatGPT "What do you know about dolphins?", you might get information about dolphin anatomy, social behavior, endangered species status, etc. If you were looking for specific information about their intelligence, for example, a more explicit instruction would have been more appropriate. Implicit instructions are a powerful tool for eliciting creative and diverse responses, but they do require some flexibility on the part of the user in terms of response expectations.

Balancing implicit and explicit instructions

The key to writing effective prompts is finding the right balance between implicit and explicit instructions. Too many explicit instructions can restrict the creativity of the language model, while too many implicit instructions can lead to imprecise or unexpected responses.

The ideal balance depends on your specific objective. If you need a precise, specific answer, it's best to give explicit instructions. If you want a more open and creative response, or are exploring a topic without specific expectations, implicit instructions may be more appropriate.

To help you understand and master the use of implicit and explicit instructions, try writing prompts for various situations using both types of instructions. For example, try writing a prompt that asks for an analysis of George Orwell's novel '1984' using explicit instructions first, then implicit instructions. Compare the answers you get and think about how the different types of instructions influence the response.

Mastering implicit and explicit instructions will help you become a more competent prompt engineer and give you more control over the responses you get from ChatGPT. So feel free to experiment and practice - and have fun doing it!

Manipulating tone and style

Manipulating tone and style in your prompts can be extremely effective in directing the AI's response and adapting it to your specific needs. Whether writing an academic paper, designing a video game dialogue or answering a question in a customer service context, tone and style are key elements to consider. They define not only how information is communicated, but also how it is received by the listener or reader.

Understanding tone and style

Tone refers to the attitude or emotion the author conveys through the way he or she writes. It can be serious, humorous, formal, informal, respectful, cheeky, optimistic, pessimistic and so on. Style, on the other hand, is the way something is written. It is the author's individual expression, influenced by word choice, sentence structure, rhythm, grammatical voice, and many other elements.

Tone manipulation

When formulating a prompt, specifying the tone you want the AI to adopt can help tailor the response to your needs. For example, if you want the AI to write a blog post on a serious topic, you might ask: "Write a blog post on climate change, adopting a serious and concerned tone."

Similarly, if you want the AI to answer a question on an online forum, you might want it to adopt a friendly, informal tone. For example, you might ask, "How would you explain relativity to a five-year-old child, adopting a friendly and simple tone?"

Style manipulation

Specifying the style can also be useful for getting the right response. For example, if you want the AI to generate a story, you can ask: "Tell an adventure story in the style of J.R.R. Tolkien". Similarly, if you want a descriptive text, you could ask: "Describe a sunrise in the poetic style of Robert Frost".

Limits and challenges

However, it's important to understand that although GPT is capable of mimicking different tones and styles to some degree, it does have its limitations. It cannot perfectly reproduce the style of a specific author, and it may not always correctly interpret the desired tone.

Manipulating tone and style in your prompts can be a powerful tool for getting answers tailored to your specific needs. By practicing and experimenting, you can hone your ability to use these techniques effectively. However, bear in mind the limitations of AI and don't hesitate to iterate and tweak your prompts to get the results you want.

The art of writing prompts for artificial intelligence is an exciting journey of exploration and discovery, littered with successes as well as challenges. As we progress on this journey, we learn to understand and manipulate the crucial elements that shape AI responses, such as tone and style. We learn to instruct the AI not only on what we want it to do, but also on how we want it to do it. We guide the AI to adopt tones ranging from serious to friendly, from formal to informal. We invite it to borrow the styles of great writers, to weave stories in the wake of J.R.R. Tolkien, or to paint pictures with words in the manner of Robert Frost.

But this journey is not without its obstacles. We've learned that while GPT is capable of mimicking different tones and styles to some degree, it does have its limitations. It can't perfectly reproduce the style of a specific author, and it may not always correctly interpret the desired tone. We've discovered that the challenge lies not only in formulating the ideal prompt, but also in understanding the capabilities and limitations of the AI we're interacting with.

And yet, these challenges in no way diminish the value of this journey. On the contrary, they enrich our experience, pushing us to experiment, iterate and refine. Every interaction with the AI is an opportunity to learn and grow, a chance to become more adept at the art of writing prompts.

Ultimately, manipulating tone and style in your prompts is more than just a tool for getting answers tailored to your specific needs. It's a valuable skill that allows you to explore the potential of AI in a deeper, more meaningful way. It's a pathway to transforming your interactions with AI into a creative and enriching dialogue. Keep practicing, keep experimenting, keep learning, and you'll discover a world of endless possibilities in the fascinating world of AI-based language models.

-11-

Perfecting prompts

"AI will help us free humanity from repetitive tasks."

Kai-Fu Lee

In the ever-changing world of artificial intelligence, the ability to interact effectively with language models is a valuable skill. It's an art that requires a thorough understanding of language models, as well as meticulous attention to the wording and intent of your prompts. However, even the most skilled among us are not immune to the common and subtle errors that can creep into our interaction with language models like ChatGPT. Understanding these common errors, recognizing them when they occur and learning how to avoid them can greatly improve the quality of our interactions with these systems.

The art of formulating prompts is a delicate balance. On the one hand, there's the danger of vague or open-ended wording. When instructions are too general or lack specific details, the responses generated by the language model can deviate from what we had in mind. On the other hand, there is the danger of making erroneous assumptions about the knowledge or understanding of the language model. These systems, despite their ability to generate responses that appear to contain knowledge or understanding, in reality have no awareness of what they "know". They are simply programmed to generate responses based on the information they have received during their training.

So, as we prepare to dive deeper into the world of prompt formulation, we need to keep these common pitfalls in mind. We'll explore examples of vague or open-ended wording, which, while they may seem harmless at first, can lead to unpredictable or unaligned responses. We'll also examine the consequences of making erroneous assumptions about knowledge or experience of the language model, a mistake that can lead to misunderstanding and unnecessary confusion. Through this exploration, we'll learn how to formulate prompts that are more efficient, accurate and aligned with our intentions, in order to make the most of our interactions with AI-based language models.

Common pitfalls in prompt design

Effective prompt design is an art that requires both a clear understanding of the underlying language model and the ability to anticipate possible responses. However, even the most experienced prompt designers can fall into some common pitfalls. These errors are often subtle and may not be obvious at first glance. That's why it's important to be aware of them and learn how to avoid them.

Vagabonding in formulation

One of the most common pitfalls in designing prompts is vague or open-ended wording. Language models, like ChatGPT, are designed to generate responses based on the input they receive. If your prompt is vague, the language model could produce a response that isn't aligned with what you had in mind. It is therefore necessary to be as precise and detailed as possible in your prompt.

For example, instead of asking the AI to "Write me a story", try giving more details, such as "Write me a science fiction story set in a colony on Mars".

Erroneous assumptions about model knowledge

Another common trap is to assume that the language model has some knowledge or experience that it doesn't have. It's essential to remember that language models, while capable of generating responses that appear to contain knowledge or understanding, actually have no awareness of what they "know". They simply generate responses based on the information they have received during their training.

For example, asking ChatGPT "What's your favorite book?" is an ill-conceived prompt, as it assumes that the model has preferences, which it doesn't. A more appropriate formulation might be "Which book is often recommended for learning programming?".

Excessive prompt length

The temptation to provide excessive detail in your prompt may be strong, especially if you're trying to get a very specific response. However, prompts that are too long or too detailed can actually harm the quality of the response. They can confuse the model or steer it in a direction you hadn't intended. A good rule of thumb is to keep your prompts as short and concise as possible, while providing enough detail to guide the model towards the desired response.

Poor expectation management

A final pitfall to avoid is mismanaging your expectations when it comes to language model performance. Although models like ChatGPT are incredibly advanced and capable of generating very convincing responses, they aren't perfect and can sometimes give incorrect, inconsistent or confusing answers. It's important to bear this in mind and not expect the template to always generate the "right" response to your prompts.

Ultimately, effective prompt design is a constant learning process. By avoiding these common pitfalls and constantly refining your prompts based on the feedback you receive, you can dramatically improve the quality of the responses you get from your language model.

Problem-solving strategies

When working with language models such as ChatGPT, you can sometimes encounter unexpected challenges. Your prompt may not generate the response you expected, or the output could be ambiguous or off-topic. In such scenarios, it's important to have a toolbox of problem-solving strategies to help you refine your prompts and get the results you want.

Understanding the problem

The first step in problem solving is to clearly understand the problem. This means carefully analyzing the answer generated by the language model and identifying areas where it falls short. Is there a lack of precision in the answer? Is the information incorrect or misinterpreted? Has the AI completely ignored part of your prompt? By identifying the problem, you can start to develop a strategy for dealing with it.

Prompt reformulation

Once you've identified the problem, a common strategy is to rephrase your prompt. For example, if you find that the answer is too vague, you can try making your prompt more specific. If the AI seems to ignore part of your prompt, you can try making that part more explicit or presenting it differently.

Tone and style guidance

Sometimes, the problem may lie not in the content of the reply, but in its tone or style. In this case, you can use your prompt to guide the AI more explicitly. For example, you might ask the AI to "respond as if explaining the topic to a five-year-old" or to "write a formal response suitable for an academic report". By guiding tone and style, you can get the AI to produce a response more appropriate to your context.

Add context

In some cases, adding more context to your prompt can help solve problems. For example, if you ask the AI to "write a cover letter for a job application", ChatGPT might generate a fairly generic letter. However, if you add "write a cover letter for a job application as a software developer in an IT startup", the AI now has much more context to generate a more precise and relevant response.

Iteration and experimentation

Finally, it's important to remember that problem-solving with prompts is often an iterative process. You may need to try several different rephrasings, adjust your tone and style, or add more context before you find the solution that works for your particular situation. Experimentation is key, and each trial will give you more information to refine your approach.

Overall, problem solving with prompts is an essential aspect of prompt engineering. By developing a solid understanding of the language model, learning to identify and understand problems, and acquiring a range of strategies for dealing with them, you can become a skilled and effective prompt engineer.

Summary of the prompt improvement process

Prompt formulation is a skill that improves with time and practice. It's not a linear process where a perfect idea emerges from the first try. On the contrary, improving prompts is an iterative process, often requiring several cycles of design, testing, analysis and revision. Here's how it works.

Understanding the iterative process

First, it's important to understand that designing prompts is not an exact science. AI models like ChatGPT are extremely powerful tools, but they're not perfect. They have strengths and weaknesses, and they won't always react in the way you expect. So it's important to give yourself permission to experiment, to make mistakes, and to learn from them.

The aim of the iterative process is to gradually arrive at a prompt version that delivers the desired results. This is achieved through a series of adjustments and improvements, each based on lessons learned from previous trials.

Stage 1: Initial prompt design

The initial design of the prompt is your starting point. You can start with a general idea of what you want the AI to do, and then formulate a prompt that you think will achieve that goal. At this stage, it's important to take notes on your intentions and expectations, as these will form the basis of your analysis later on.

Step 2: The prompt test

Once you've designed your initial prompt, it's time to test it. Put the prompt to the AI and observe the results. It's important to note that you shouldn't just focus on whether the answer is "correct" or "incorrect". You also need to examine how the AI arrived at that answer, and what aspects of the prompt influenced the result.

Step 3: Analysis of results

Once you've tested your prompt, take time to analyze the results. Examine the AI's response and compare it with your initial expectations. What went well? What failed? Were there aspects of the prompt that the AI misinterpreted, or information that it ignored? Take detailed notes on your observations.

Stage 4: Prompt revision

Based on your analysis, revise your prompt. Try adjusting the parts that didn't work as you'd hoped, or adding more detail to guide the AI towards the desired response. It can also be useful to test different formulations or structures of prompts to see if they give better results.

Once you've revised your prompt, go back to step 2 and repeat the process. With each iteration, you'll get closer and closer to the ideal answer.

Demonstrate patience and perseverance

Improving prompts is a process that requires patience and perseverance. It's rare to find the "perfect prompt" on the first try. However, by engaging in this iterative process, learning from your mistakes, and constantly striving to do better, you can dramatically improve your prompt design skills.

Every effort you make to improve your prompts is an investment in your ability to work with AI. Every lesson you learn in the process will make you more competent and confident in your ability to direct AI towards the results you want to achieve. And over time, you'll find that you're able to create more effective prompts, more quickly, and with less effort. That's the real power of the iterative process of improving prompts.

Improving prompts is a process that requires patience and perseverance. It's rare to find the "perfect prompt" on the first try. However, by engaging in this iterative process, learning from your mistakes, and constantly striving to do better, you can dramatically improve your prompt design skills.

Every effort you make to improve your prompts is an investment in your ability to work with AI. Every lesson you learn in the process will make you more competent and confident in your ability to direct AI towards the results you want to achieve. And over time, you'll find that you're able to create more effective prompts, more quickly, and with less effort. That's the real power of the iterative process of improving prompts.

The evolution of AI and machine learning models such as GPT-4 and beyond has elevated the importance of effective prompt design. With the increasing power of these models comes an escalating need for precision in guiding their output. An improperly formulated prompt can lead to outcomes that range from slightly off-target to entirely unhelpful or even misleading. Thus, the art and science of crafting effective prompts have become paramount for those working at the forefront of AI applications.

To truly appreciate the value of refining prompts, it's essential to understand the vast landscape of applications for AI. From crafting bespoke marketing content to conducting complex data analyses, predicting global trends, or generating creative arts, the potential applications are boundless. In each of these arenas, the quality of the AI's output hinges significantly on the quality of the input – the prompt.

For instance, consider a business analyst who uses AI to forecast market trends. A vague or imprecise prompt might lead the AI to generate general or untargeted predictions. But, with a well-crafted prompt that accurately captures the nuances of the analyst's query, the AI can produce insights that are both actionable and specific, offering the business a competitive advantage.

Beyond professional applications, the ability to formulate effective prompts significantly affects personal interactions with AI. As AI integrates more deeply into our everyday lives – from personal assistants to smart home devices – being able to communicate our needs clearly and efficiently becomes increasingly crucial.

However, mastering prompt design is not just about achieving the desired output. It's also about understanding and navigating the underlying intricacies of the AI model. It involves a deep dive into the mechanics of language, cognition, and even empathy. The best prompts often bridge the gap between cold, machine computation and human warmth and nuance. They recognize that while AI operates on data, its most valuable outputs often intersect with human emotion, intent, and context.

Moreover, the iterative process of improving prompts instills in the designer a growth mindset. Each failure becomes a stepping stone, each misstep an opportunity for growth. This mindset not only benefits prompt design but also translates into other areas of work and life. It encourages resilience, adaptability, and continuous learning – qualities that are invaluable in an ever-evolving digital landscape.

As AI models continue to grow in complexity, the challenge of crafting the "perfect prompt" might become more demanding. However, the principles of patience, learning, and iterative improvement will remain constant. The designers who internalize these principles will be the ones who stay ahead of the curve, harnessing the full potential of AI to drive innovation.

Furthermore, improved prompt design can also be a significant career differentiator. As organizations increasingly rely on AI to inform decision-making, individuals adept at interfacing with these tools will be in high demand. They'll be viewed as invaluable assets, not just for their technical proficiency, but also for their ability to translate complex requirements into actionable AI-driven insights.

It's also worth noting the ethical dimension of prompt design. As AI finds its way into more critical applications, ensuring that it acts in ways that are ethical, fair, and just becomes paramount. A well-designed prompt can be the difference between an AI that perpetuates bias and one that challenges it, between an AI that misinforms and one that enlightens. Thus, mastering the craft of prompt design is not just a technical challenge; it's a moral imperative.

-12-

Practical applications of prompt engineering

"The real question of AI is not 'when will it happen?", but 'how well will we use it?'"

James Manyika

Case studies from industry and academia

In this chapter, we'll explore several real-life use cases of designing prompts for AI language models, both in industry and academia. These case studies illustrate not only the variety of possible applications for prompts, but also the unique challenges that each scenario can present.

1. Assistance in drafting industry e-mails

A Silicon Valley startup has developed a GPT-3-based tool to assist users in writing e-mails. The aim was to provide users with suggestions for completing their sentences while writing e-mails. The challenge lay in formulating prompts that could give useful, relevant and contextually correct suggestions. The company succeeded in developing a set of rules for creating prompts that significantly improved the quality of the AI's suggestions. Ultimately, this tool helped many professionals save time and write more effective e-mails.

2. Automatic content generation in the academic world

A team of researchers at a leading university used GPT-3 to automatically generate content for an online course. They formulated prompts to produce explanations of complex concepts, examples of problems, and even quizzes to test students' understanding. Although automatic content generation presented challenges, such as verifying the accuracy and relevance of information, the team succeeded in developing an iteration and verification process that produced quality content. This project not only saved time and resources in content creation, but also demonstrated the potential of AI for education.

3. Data analysis in industry

A data science consultancy has used prompts to help analyze large text datasets. Using GPT-3, they were able to generate summaries, trend analyses and data insights automatically. The challenge lay in creating prompts that could direct the AI towards meaningful analyses while avoiding errors or biases. Through a process of fine-tuning and iteration, the company was able to develop a set of techniques for creating prompts that improved the efficiency and accuracy of their analyses.

4. Supporting language learning in the academic world

In a university research project, a team used GPT-3 to develop a language learning application. By formulating prompts to generate language practice exercises, simulated conversations and grammar explanations, they succeeded in creating an interactive learning resource for students. Although ensuring accuracy and cultural relevance posed challenges, the team succeeded in developing an approach to creating prompts that overcame these obstacles.

Each of these case studies offers valuable insights into the art of creating prompts. They demonstrate that while designing prompts can be challenging, a careful and considered approach can make the most of the capabilities of AI language models.

The use of prompts in creative writing and art

Artistic creation is often seen as a mystical process, a complex alchemy of inspiration, skill and vision. This fusion of tangible and intangible factors brings new and unique ideas to life. Yet, at the heart of this whirlwind of creativity, artificial intelligence has proved to be a valuable addition, offering artists and writers a powerful tool to stimulate and realize their creative ideas.

Language models, such as OpenAI's ChatGPT, have been specifically designed to generate text from prompts. But beyond this ability to produce text, they offer invaluable potential for artistic creation. Whether writing a novel, composing a play, directing a film, creating a work of art, or even developing a video game, ChatGPT prompts can be used to generate ideas, explore concepts, and serve as a springboard for creativity.

In this section, we'll explore in depth the different ways AI can be used in the field of art and creativity. We'll start by looking at how ChatGPT prompts can be used to generate ideas for creative writing. For example, a blocked author might use a prompt to generate ideas for a new character, a novel plot, or even a particularly difficult turn of phrase.

Next, we'll look at how AI can help create original content. Indeed, with the right guidance, a language model like ChatGPT can help write film scripts, video game scripts, play dialogues, and many other forms of written content. And while these AI-generated texts often require refinement by a human writer, they can nevertheless serve as a solid starting point.

Finally, we'll look at how AI can pave the way for new forms of artistic expression. With techniques such as text-to-image, where AI transforms a textual description into an image, artists can explore new creative horizons, combining words and visuals in innovative ways.

So, as AI continues to evolve and perfect itself, its role as a tool in the process of artistic creation only grows stronger. Far from being a threat to human creativity, it rather offers a range of opportunities, opening the door to new ways of thinking, creating and expressing our vision of the world.

AI as a source of inspiration

In the creative field, whether writing a novel, composing a symphony, or creating a new work of art, one of the greatest obstacles a creator can face is creative block. That dreaded moment when, despite our best efforts, ideas simply seem to run out. It's something every designer has experienced at one time or another, and it can be incredibly frustrating. However, artificial intelligence, and in particular language models like ChatGPT, offer a promising solution to this dilemma.

A well-formulated prompt, passed on to a language model, can generate a host of new and unexpected ideas. In the example given, the user might ask ChatGPT to "create a summary for a science fiction story that involves time travel and dinosaurs". In doing so, the user doesn't simply dictate the scenario to the AI, but rather gives it a general framework, a creative space in which the AI can explore and generate unique ideas.

The genius of this approach lies in the fact that language models like ChatGPT have no opinions, prejudices or creative restrictions. They are not limited by what has been done before, or by what is considered "possible" or "realistic". They are capable of generating ideas that might be totally unexpected, even absurd to a human mind.

The results generated by the AI can then be used as a starting point for a new work. For example, the summary of the science fiction story could inspire an author to write a novel, a play, or even a film script. Similarly, an AI-generated idea for a musical composition could serve as the spark for a new piece of music.

Ultimately, AI is not a threat to human creativity, but rather a powerful tool that can stimulate it. By generating a plethora of new and unexpected ideas, AI can help break down the barriers of creative block, broaden our perspective and inspire us to create works of art that surpass the limits of our imagination.

AI as co-creator

In the ever-expanding world of Artificial Intelligence, we've gone from looking askance at cold, distant technology to celebrating a new partner in the creative process: AI as co-creator. This concept, which once seemed worthy of science fiction, is now a tangible reality thanks to language models like ChatGPT, designed by OpenAI. Thanks to their prodigious text generation capabilities, these models have redefined the landscape of content creation, expanding the horizons of what is possible.

ChatGPT's ability to generate ideas is just the first step in a deeper collaboration. Indeed, AI can help not only to spark ideas, but also to develop these ideas into original and complete content. Take fiction writing, for example. Writing a story from scratch can be a daunting task, even for the most seasoned writers. ChatGPT, however, can help overcome this initial block by generating a first draft based on a simple prompt, providing a solid foundation from which the writer can continue to develop and refine his or her work.

The use of AI is not limited to writing prose. Screenwriters, for example, can use ChatGPT to generate dialogue for their scripts. By providing a prompt describing the characters, the context and the general direction of the conversation, AI can generate realistic and captivating dialogues, allowing screenwriters to concentrate on the overall plot and character dynamics.

In addition, visual artists can also benefit from AI text generation. ChatGPT can create evocative descriptions of artworks, helping artists to communicate their vision and engage audiences in a deeper way. A well-formulated prompt, describing the artwork and the feelings the artist wishes to evoke, can lead the AI to produce a powerful, poetic description that adds an extra dimension to the artistic experience.

The heart of this new co-creation paradigm lies in the ability to direct AI with appropriate prompts to produce content that matches your style and vision. This guided direction does not hinder the creativity of the model; on the contrary, it results in content that is both relevant and personalized, reflecting the unique intersection of artificial intelligence and human creativity. Thus, we see that AI is not a threat to human creativity, but rather a tool that amplifies it, offering new possibilities for creative expression and content generation.

AI as critic and reviewer

Artificial intelligence not only has the potential to help create new and exciting work, it can also play an important role in the revision and improvement process. Language models like ChatGPT can serve as powerful editing tools, offering suggestions for refining and improving existing content.

Take the work of a writer, for example. After writing an initial draft, a writer might ask ChatGPT to provide suggestions for improving a specific paragraph. The AI might suggest rewordings to improve clarity, suggest synonyms to enrich vocabulary, or even restructure sentences to improve narrative flow.

Similarly, in the context of script dialogue or a play, AI can help revise exchanges to make them sound more natural and authentic. For example, you could ask ChatGPT to "Revise this dialogue to make it sound more natural between two 21st century teenagers". The AI could then suggest modifications that reflect current teenage ways of speaking, making the dialogue more realistic for contemporary audiences.

Even in the field of art, AI can be used as a critic. On the basis of a textual description of a work of art, you can ask ChatGPT to evaluate or criticize the work. Although the AI can't "see" the artwork, it can analyze the text of the description and generate a critique based on known art standards and trends. Of course, it should be noted that AI's suggestions and critiques are based on automated learning models and not on subjective feelings or experiences. It won't replace human judgment or the expertise of a professional art critic, but it can provide insights and suggestions that might otherwise go unnoticed.

It's also important to bear in mind that while AI can provide interesting suggestions and critiques, it's no substitute for human judgment. Creativity, art and writing are deeply human expressions, and AI cannot (at least not yet) capture all the nuances and subtleties that we, as human beings, put into our work. However, used wisely, AI can be a valuable tool for enhancing and refining our creations, adding another layer of depth and sophistication to our work.

Mastering prompts for artistic creation

Creating effective prompts for creative writing and art requires a certain amount of skill. It's important to give the AI a clear direction while leaving room for creativity. A good prompt should guide the AI, but not be so specific that it limits creative possibilities.

Art and creative writing are fields that benefit greatly from the introduction of AI, and more specifically from the use of well-designed prompts. As AI continues to develop and improve, the opportunities for artists and writers to collaborate with AI and create unique and innovative works will only grow.

The role of prompts in data analysis

There are many applications for prompts in data analysis, from generating trend descriptions to forecasting time series. Language models, such as ChatGPT, can interact with data in incredibly flexible ways, producing meaningful information that may not be immediately obvious.

First, let's consider the use of prompts for generating trend descriptions. Let's say you have a large temporal data set, such as the price variations of a stock over several years. You could use a prompt to ask the AI to generate a description of price trends over this period. For example, you could write: "ChatGPT, describe the general share price trends of company X between 2015 and 2023." With appropriate upstream data analysis, ChatGPT could then generate a detailed and comprehensible description of the key trends in these prices.

In another application, you could use a prompt to ask ChatGPT to predict a time series. Although the AI is not specifically designed for predicting time series, it could nevertheless provide a rough approximation. An example prompt in this case might be, "ChatGPT, gives a rough forecast of the direction of company X's stock price for the next quarter, based on trends over the past two years."

In addition, prompts can be used to generate reports from data. For example, you might have a large dataset from a customer satisfaction survey. You could ask ChatGPT to generate a summary of the survey results, using a prompt like, "AI, summarizes the main points of dissatisfaction expressed by customers in this survey." ChatGPT could then analyze the survey data and produce a detailed, informative summary.

Finally, it's also possible to use prompts to generate questions to ask your dataset. For example, if you have a large dataset and you're not sure what information you want to extract from it, you could ask the AI to generate a list of interesting questions to ask your dataset. For example, you could write: "ChatGPT, give a list of interesting questions to ask about the share price trends of company X over the last five years."

Prompts play an essential role in data analysis, enabling complex questions to be asked, trends to be explored, reports to be generated and even the future to be predicted. As the field of artificial intelligence continues to develop, the potential of prompts in data analysis will only grow. As a prompts engineer, it's essential to understand and exploit this potential to extract maximum value from your data.

-13-

The future of prompt engineering

"We have to realize that AI is not the future, but the present."

Sebastian Thrun

We stand at a pivotal moment in technological history, where artificial intelligence is shaping and redefining the way we interact with the world around us. Language models, such as ChatGPT, have become an integral part of our daily lives, and continue to evolve at a speed that was unimaginable just a decade ago. In this context, the way we interact and formulate prompts to these patterns is of paramount importance. As we navigate this ever-changing technological landscape, it is necessary to anticipate and understand future developments in AI, in order to continue to refine and perfect the art of prompt engineering.

In the following sections, we dive into some of the most promising developments in the field of AI that could change the way we interact with language models. We'll explore the potential advent of explanatory AI, which aims to make the AI response generation process more transparent and understandable. We will also consider the possible impact of advances towards real-time AI, which would enable more fluid and natural interactions with language models.

In addition, we'll look at the prospects of personalized AI, where language models could be tailored to the specific needs of particular individuals or groups. In addition, as artificial intelligence gains in power and ubiquity, questions of ethics and responsibility become increasingly important, and we'll touch on some of the important discussions on the horizon in this area.

In parallel, we'll be detailing the rapid evolution of the field of prompt engineering, highlighting how practices and techniques have changed and continue to transform over time. In short, we're about to embark on an exciting journey through the future of AI and prompt engineering, a journey that promises to be as rewarding as it is inspiring. Hold on to your hats, because the future of AI has many surprises in store for us.

Future developments in AI

As we dive into the fascinating world of AI, it's important to keep an eye on the horizon. Advances in artificial intelligence are evolving at an incredibly rapid pace, and what was once considered science fiction is now an everyday reality. In this section, we explore some of the most promising upcoming developments in AI, and how they could shape the art and science of prompt engineering.

Explanatory AI

Language models, such as ChatGPT, have demonstrated an impressive level of effectiveness in a wide range of application areas, from generating text responses in chat systems, through content creation support, to article writing. However, much of their inner workings remain a mystery to us. Indeed, these systems, though prodigiously powerful, are often perceived as "black boxes". We submit a prompt to them and they produce an answer, but the precise process by which they generate that answer often remains opaque, hidden behind layers of complex algorithms and huge amounts of data.

In the face of this challenge, explanatory AI is emerging as a promising area of research. The aim of explanatory AI is to decipher these opaque processes and make them more transparent and comprehensible to humans. This means that, in the future, it might be possible to ask a language model not only to produce a response, but also to explain how and why it produced that specific response. This explanation could involve breaking down the model's reasoning, identifying the data on which it relied, and even showing how it evaluated different potential answers before choosing the one it generated.

For example, in a teaching context, an explanatory language model might not only solve a math problem, but also detail the steps it took to arrive at the solution. This could help students understand not only the solution itself, but also the thought process that led to that solution.

Explanatory AI could also play an important role in AI trust and accountability. If a language model makes a recommendation or decision, it's important to understand why it made that decision, especially if that decision has significant consequences. Explanatory AI can help provide this understanding, enabling users to better understand, evaluate and, if necessary, challenge decisions made by artificial intelligence.

Nevertheless, it should be noted that explanatory artificial intelligence is a fast-growing field of research, and much remains to be done to realize its full potential. The challenges are many, ranging from the inherent complexity of language models, to the difficulty of translating algorithmic processes into explanations understandable to humans. However, despite these challenges, explanatory AI promises to open up a new way of making artificial intelligence more transparent, understandable and ultimately more useful to everyone.

AI in real time

In today's technological landscape, most interactions with language models, such as ChatGPT, take place via static text. The process is fairly simple and linear: we submit a prompt, wait for the AI to generate a response, then submit another prompt based on the response received. While this form of interaction has led to significant advances in the way we use AI, there's an additional dimension that's starting to be explored and has the potential to fundamentally transform the way we interact with these technologies: real-time artificial intelligence.

Real-time AI refers to systems where the language model interacts with users in real time, i.e. it generates responses simultaneously as it receives input from the user. This is much closer to a natural conversation, such as we would have with another human being, where exchanges are fluid and responses are generated instantaneously based on the input received.

This breakthrough could have major implications in many fields. For example, in customer services, real-time AI could handle customer queries in a much more efficient and personalized way, generating instant responses based on information provided by the customer. In education, it could be used to create virtual tutors who can interact with students in real time, answering their questions and guiding them through complex problems as they encounter them.

There are also fascinating implications for the field of entertainment. Imagine a video game where non-player characters are powered by AI in real time, able to react and adapt instantly to your in-game actions. Or a virtual reality application where AI can interact with you in real time, creating an immersive experience that looks more and more like the real thing.

Of course, real-time AI also presents challenges, not least in terms of the computing and processing resources required to produce real-time responses. However, with rapid advances in computer and AI technology, it's likely that we'll see more and more real-time AI applications in the near future. This is an exciting frontier to explore, and it has the potential to transform our interaction with AI in fundamental and lasting ways.

Personalized AI

Personalized artificial intelligence, a technology that is still emerging, but whose implications are enormous, suggests a transition to a future where AIs are even more aligned with individual needs. Until now, the majority of language models, such as ChatGPT, have been trained on general data drawn from the Internet, books, articles and other sources. As a result, they produce generic answers designed to be useful to a wide variety of users. It's a necessarily broad approach, but it doesn't allow for the level of personalized interaction that might be possible with more sophisticated systems.

In fact, the future could see the emergence of personalized language models, tailored to the specific needs of each individual or group of users. Imagine a personal assistant who, after being trained on your past correspondence, writings and preferences, would be able to respond exactly the way you want. This could go beyond simply understanding your writing style or conversational preferences. Such a system could include your own cultural references, inside jokes, and even your way of thinking.

What's more, a customized model could have a significant impact in the professional world. For example, a company could train a language model on its own internal documentation, enabling the AI to understand and align with company-specific terminologies, work processes and even corporate culture. This could lead to AI that is not just a conversational assistant, but a true collaborator, capable of providing relevant and useful contributions in a professional context.

It's important to note that this advanced personalization raises important questions about data privacy and security. After all, for a language model to be truly personalized, it must be trained on very personal data. This is a challenge that researchers and engineers need to take into account when designing these personalized systems.

Personalized AI, with its potential for more natural and relevant interaction, can change the way we interact with technology. It's a rapidly developing area that deserves particular attention as we look to the future of conversational language models.

AI and ethics

Finally, AI and ethics is an area that will undoubtedly receive increased attention in the future. As AI becomes more powerful and ubiquitous, questions about how to use AI ethically and responsibly become increasingly important. This includes questions about data privacy and security, AI transparency, fairness and non-discrimination, and accountability for AI's actions.

In short, the future of AI is both exciting and uncertain. As Prompt Engineers, we have the unique opportunity to be at the forefront of these developments, to learn and grow with AI as it continues to evolve. It's a journey that requires curiosity, flexibility, and a constant willingness to learn and adapt - but it's also a journey that's sure to be exciting, challenging, and incredibly rewarding.

Evolution of prompt engineering practices

In the future, we can expect prompt engineering to continue to evolve at a steady pace. As the capabilities of language models like GPT-4 and beyond increase, users will be able to interact with AI in even more natural and intuitive ways. Prompts could become more complex and nuanced, reflecting the richness and depth of human communication.

At the same time, the importance of prompt engineering is likely to be recognized and integrated into a wider range of disciplines. For example, in education, teachers could use prompt engineering to create personalized interactive learning exercises. In marketing and advertising, professionals could use prompt engineering to generate attractive and relevant promotional content.

It's also likely that we'll see more and more applications where prompts are generated and adjusted automatically by algorithms. This could enable greater personalization and efficiency, but it also raises important questions about ethics and transparency.

In this context, the role of prompt engineers will not only be to formulate effective prompts, but also to navigate these ethical challenges and help establish responsible standards and practices. They will not only need to understand how AI works, but also how it can be used in a way that respects users' values and rights.

Finally, as we move towards a future where AI is an integral part of our daily lives, prompt engineering may well become a key competency. Individuals, companies and institutions that master this skill will be well placed to make the most of the advantages offered by AI-based language models.

The impact of User Expectations

As we move further into the age of artificial intelligence, user expectations of AI-based language models like ChatGPT continue to evolve and intensify. Users are no longer simply looking to interact with a system that generates generic answers; they expect a personalized, relevant and dynamic experience that can truly understand and respond to their specific needs. This growing need for more precise, relevant and creative responses fuels a constant search for new strategies and techniques to improve prompt formulation.

Users' expectations are not limited to the accuracy and relevance of the answers generated. They are also looking for greater interactivity and a better understanding of their intentions, moods and desires. Consequently, the ability of language models to interpret and respond to a wider range of signals and nuances in prompts is becoming increasingly important.

Users also expect AI to respect their values and sensitivities. They want language models that can adapt to their communication style, reflect their values and avoid inappropriate or offensive responses. What's more, as privacy and data security issues become increasingly important, users expect language models to respect their privacy and protect their personal information.

Finally, users increasingly expect language models to be able to learn and adapt over time. They want their past experiences with the model to inform future interactions, enabling AI to better understand and respond to their specific needs.

In short, user expectations for the future of prompt engineering are high. They require constant innovation, ongoing research and agile adaptation to changing user needs. These expectations are shaping the evolution of prompt engineering, pushing the technology to new heights of relevance, personalization and understanding.

The Future of Prompts Engineering

In the future, we can expect to see prompt engineering continue to evolve in response to technological developments, user expectations and emerging challenges.

A likely area of evolution is the integration of prompt engineering with other AI techniques, such as reinforcement learning, to create systems that can learn and adapt based on user feedback.

Furthermore, as language models become increasingly capable of understanding context, we could see the emergence of contextual prompts, which draw on the model's knowledge of the situation or user to generate more relevant responses.

Finally, prompt engineering could also evolve to meet ethical challenges, such as the need to generate answers that are not only accurate and useful, but also fair and privacy-friendly.

Overall, the evolution of prompt engineering practices illustrates the dynamics and excitement of this growing field. It's certain that prompt engineers will continue to innovate and push the boundaries of what AI-based language models can achieve.

Ethical considerations and best practices

As we venture further into the new frontier of artificial intelligence, questions of ethics and responsibility take on paramount importance. The formulation of prompts for language models such as ChatGPT is no exception. As our interaction with these systems deepens, we need to be aware of the potential impacts of our work. This chapter looks at some of the key ethical considerations and presents recommended best practices in the field.

Privacy awareness

As we move further into the digital age, the issue of privacy awareness takes on increasing importance. As we integrate more technology, including artificial intelligence, into our daily lives, we need to be increasingly vigilant about how our personal information is used and protected.

In this context, it's essential to remember that, although language models like GPT-4 are capable of generating incredibly realistic and convincing responses, they don't know any specific or confidential information about individuals. They are trained on a wide range of publicly available texts, and have no access to specific personal data unless this is explicitly provided to them during the interaction.

That said, it's important never to ask a language model to obtain, store or disclose personally identifiable information. This also extends to the need to avoid sharing sensitive information with the AI, even if it doesn't store it permanently. Because even if the AI itself is unable to misuse this information, human error or security breaches can potentially put this information at risk.

In the future, we could see an evolution in the way language models handle confidential information. Advances in privacy technologies, such as federated learning and differential privacy, could enable language models to be trained in such a way that they can learn sensitive information without ever directly accessing that information. This could lead to language models that can provide even more personalized and relevant responses, while protecting user confidentiality.

Privacy awareness will continue to be an important topic as we move forward into this new era of conversational AI. It will require a combination of technological advances, user education and effective regulations to ensure that we can make the most of these powerful tools while respecting and protecting our right to privacy.

Responsible use

In the future evolution of the responsible use of AI, a key dimension will be to ensure a balance between the transformational potential of this technology and the need to prevent and mitigate potential abuses. As language models such as GPT become more powerful and ubiquitous, the question of their responsible use becomes increasingly relevant.

Beyond current recommendations, which encourage avoiding the creation of prompts that incite the production of harmful, misleading or offensive content, it is likely that new ethical standards and guidelines of conduct will be developed. These new rules could include more sophisticated moderation mechanisms, based on AI itself, to monitor and control the content generated.

Another important aspect will be educating users and developers about the ethical implications of using AI. As artificial intelligence has no awareness of truth or falsehood and simply generates responses based on the data it has been trained on, it will be necessary to promote a deeper understanding of the limits and potential biases of artificial intelligence. This education could include training on how to interact responsibly with AI, as well as how to identify and report abuse.

Furthermore, a key aspect of the future evolution of the responsible use of artificial intelligence will be the development of systems of accountability and transparency. Companies and developers who create and deploy these technologies could be held to account for how they have trained their models, the data sources they have used, and the measures they have taken to prevent abuse.

In short, the future evolution of responsible AI use will require large-scale cooperation between developers, users, regulators and the communities affected by these technologies. Through education, innovation and accountability, we can work together to ensure that AI is used in a way that maximizes its benefits while minimizing its risks.

Bias compliance

In the future, respect for bias will be a central component in the evolution of artificial intelligence. Language models like GPT are designed to learn from the data they are trained on. This means that they can inherit the biases inherent in this data, be they cultural, social, ethnic or other in nature. These biases can manifest themselves in the responses generated by the AI, creating ethical and accuracy issues. For this reason, taking biases into account is an essential issue for the evolution of AI.

In the next few years, we should see increasingly sophisticated solutions to deal with these biases. This could involve the development of fairer training techniques, which take account of biases in the training data and attempt to correct them. Similarly, methods for assessing and mitigating bias in AI-generated responses could be developed, such as proofreading and correcting responses or rephrasing prompts to avoid possible bias.

In addition, the introduction of personalized learning could also help to mitigate biases. Models could be trained on user-specific data, more accurately reflecting individual values and perspectives, while minimizing the influence of general biases present in broader learning data.

However, it must be emphasized that bias compliance is not just a technical issue. It also requires awareness and involvement on the part of users and developers. It involves understanding how biases can manifest themselves in AI responses, and being prepared to question and correct these biases when they are detected. It's a challenge that requires both ethical sensitivity and a long-term commitment to fairer, more respectful AI.

Promoting inclusiveness and diversity

As we move further into the age of artificial intelligence, promoting inclusivity and diversity becomes an imperative, not just in terms of end-user representation, but also in the way we interact with AI-based technologies like ChatGPT. As these systems become more integrated into our daily lives, they have an essential role to play in fostering diversity of voice, experience and perspective.

In this context, prompts play a key role. The prompts we give to these AI systems must be designed to be inclusive and representative. This means taking care not to reinforce stereotypes or traditional gender roles in the wording of our prompts. For example, instead of asking the AI to generate a story about a "housewife", we could ask it to create a story about a "person managing a house", which doesn't presume the gender of the character.

In addition, we should seek to promote a diversity of experiences and voices in AI-generated responses. This could mean asking AI to create stories or articles that highlight under-represented perspectives, or that feature a variety of characters and experiences.

These efforts are not only important to ensure fairness and inclusivity, but can also help enrich AI interactions. An AI system that can understand and reproduce a variety of experiences and perspectives can offer a richer, more nuanced user experience. Ultimately, this can help make AI a more effective and valuable tool for all users, regardless of gender, race, age, sexual orientation or life experience.

Transparency

The future of transparency in artificial intelligence is an exciting, complex and increasingly necessary topic. With the rapid and constant evolution of AI technology, and its increasing integration into every aspect of our lives, the question of transparency is emerging as a central element of the discussion on AI ethics.

The importance of transparency is manifold. First of all, it is necessary for building trust. Users need to understand when, how and why AI is used. This is particularly important in situations where AI decisions can have a significant impact on individuals or society. For example, when AI is used for content moderation, product recommendation, or even medical diagnosis, understanding AI's decision-making process can help build trust and ensure ethical and responsible use.

Secondly, transparency is essential to ensure fairness and accountability. If users don't know how an AI makes its decisions, it becomes very difficult to hold the system accountable for its actions. AI must be transparent so that users can identify and correct any biases, inaccuracies or unfairness.

Finally, transparency is also necessary for learning and continuous improvement. By understanding how an AI works and makes decisions, researchers and developers can identify areas for improvement and work towards continuous improvement of the system.

However, achieving true transparency in AI is far from an easy task. It requires a combination of research, regulation, product design and education. Researchers must continue to develop methods to make AI algorithms more understandable and explainable. Regulators need to put laws and standards in place to ensure AI transparency. Product designers must ensure that transparency is built into product design from the outset. Finally, we need to educate the public about artificial intelligence, so that they can understand and interact with these systems in an informed way.

The future evolution of AI transparency is both a challenge and an opportunity. It's a challenge because of the technical and ethical complexity of the issue. It's an opportunity because, if done right, it can build trust in AI, foster fairness and accountability, and enable continuous improvement and learning. This is an area where we all - researchers, regulators, product designers and users - need to work together to realize its full potential.

Continuing education

Ongoing education, in the context of the rapid evolution of artificial intelligence and prompt engineering, is an imperative not only to keep up with technological advances, but also to navigate the complex ethical and societal issues that arise. As language models like GPT-4 continue to develop and gain in sophistication, it is essential to maintain a thorough understanding of the implications of their use, their strengths and their limitations.

Continuing education deepens our knowledge of AI models and their applications, helping us understand how to improve prompt engineering while remaining aware of the impact our work can have on users and society as a whole. Through conferences, webinars, online courses, research articles and other resources, we can continue to broaden our horizons and hone our skills.

In a field as interdisciplinary as AI, this education must be broad and include not only technical aspects, but also ethical, sociological and psychological considerations. For example, understanding how biases can creep into AI and how to avoid them, or how to ensure respectful use of AI that values fairness, transparency and privacy.

In addition, education continues to play a role in promoting critical thinking about the long-term implications of AI technologies. This includes analysis of unintended consequences, risk management and future scenario planning.

-14-

Understanding Chat-GPT and Gpt4

"AI is the new wave of technology. It will transform every industry."

Sundar Pichai

AI, or artificial intelligence, is a hot topic, fueled by extraordinary advances in deep learning, natural language processing (NLP), and reinforcement learning. Among these developments, language models such as GPT-4 and ChatGPT are particularly impressive. These models use machine learning techniques to generate text that is often indistinguishable from that of a human being. In this article, we'll explore how to take the use of these tools a step further, focusing on advanced strategies for maximizing their potential.

OpenAI, an artificial intelligence research organization, has developed GPT-4 and ChatGPT. GPT-4, or Generative Pretrained Transformer 4, is a language model that uses deep learning to produce text of astonishing quality. ChatGPT is a variation of this model, optimized for interactive conversations.

These models are pre-trained on a large amount of text from the Internet. During their training, they learn patterns in the language, enabling GPT-4 and ChatGPT to generate responses based on the information they have ingested during their training.

Further improving the quality of prompts

An essential aspect of using GPT-4 and ChatGPT is the formulation of prompts. A prompt is a text entry that tells the model what to talk about. For example, if you ask GPT-4 to "write an essay on the history of ancient Rome", that's the prompt.

The choice of prompt can have a significant impact on the quality of the output generated. Care must be taken to ensure that the prompt is clear and precise. If the prompt is too vague, the model response may also be vague. If the prompt is too detailed, the model may be confused or ignore certain details.

A good prompt for GPT-4 or ChatGPT should also be relevant to the context of the conversation or the purpose of the text to be generated. For example, if you want the template to generate a blog post on a specific topic, your prompt should clearly indicate the topic and format of the post.

Prompt engineering techniques

Prompt engineering involves using specific strategies to formulate prompts that maximize the quality of model output. Here are a few techniques you can use:

Progressive detail technique: This involves dividing a complex question into several simpler questions. For example, instead of asking GPT-4 to "write an essay on the history of ancient Rome", you can first ask him to "write a paragraph on the history of ancient Rome", then to "write a paragraph on the main achievements of ancient Rome", and so on.

Explicit instructions: This technique involves giving detailed instructions on the structure and format of the response. For example, if you want GPT-4 to write a blog post, you can give it instructions like "Write a 500-word blog post on the history of ancient Rome, with an introduction, three main sections and a conclusion."

Applying these models to specific tasks

GPT-4 and ChatGPT can be used for a wide variety of tasks, from content authoring to code generation and decision support. Here are just a few examples of how these models can be applied:

Content writing: GPT-4 can be used to generate content for blog posts, essays, podcast scripts, speeches, and more. ChatGPT can be used to generate dialog for video games, movie scripts, training scenarios, and other applications.

Code generation: GPT-4 can be used to generate code for various programming languages. This can be particularly useful for developers looking to automate certain tasks or get help with coding problems.

Decision support: Language models can be used to analyze information and generate summaries, key points, or recommendations. This can help business leaders, analysts, researchers and others to make informed decisions.

Language models such as GPT-4 and ChatGPT represent a major advance in the field of AI. By improving our skills in prompt engineering and understanding how to apply these models to specific tasks, we can maximize their potential and take advantage of their incredible ability to generate high-quality text.

As we continue to explore the possibilities offered by these tools, we must also remain mindful of the ethical issues and societal implications of AI. By using these tools responsibly, we can help shape a future where AI improves our lives in meaningful ways.

Here are a few practical tips to help you create effective and interesting prompts. At first, you'll need to come back to these points regularly, but that's what will help you progress. Because if you gradually master these elements of improvement, you'll make a big difference in the way you render your dialogues with conversational AIs.

Understand your goals:

Before writing a prompt, ask yourself what your objective is. Are you trying to generate creative content? Ask a specific question? Obtain information on a specific topic? Having a clear idea of what you're trying to achieve will help you formulate your prompt more effectively.

Be specific:

The more specific your prompt, the more targeted the results will be. For example, rather than asking ChatGPT to "write an article on history", you could ask to "write an article on the impact of the American Civil War on the economy of the Southern states".

Use the right format:

ChatGPT is capable of understanding a wide variety of prompt formats. Whether you're asking a question, asking ChatGPT to write a story or generate a list, make sure your prompt format matches what you want to achieve.

Guide the length of the answer:

If you want a long, detailed answer, indicate this in your prompt. For example, you could ask ChatGPT to "write a detailed 500-word summary of the most important events of the Second World War".

Take inspiration from successful prompts:

Take a look at examples of prompts that have produced high-quality results. You can find them online, in forums, blogs or articles. These examples can give you ideas on how to formulate your own prompts.

Experiment:

Don't be afraid to try out different prompts and explore different query types. You may be surprised by the results you get, and discover new prompt ideas along the way.

Learn from your mistakes:

If a prompt is not producing the desired results, try to understand why and adjust it accordingly. This can help you improve your prompt formulation skills.

Think of the end user:

If you're creating prompts for an application or service, think about the end-user experience. What are they looking for? What would be the best way to formulate the prompt to get a response that meets their needs?

Consider tone and style

The wording of your prompt can influence not only the content of the response, but also the tone and style. For example, if you want the AI to write a formal, academic paragraph, your prompt should reflect this tone. Conversely, if you want a more casual or humorous response, your prompt should indicate this.

Educating AI

Don't underestimate the power of direct instruction in your prompt. Sometimes, to get the desired result, you may need to explicitly ask the AI to think, reason or imagine in a certain way. For example, if you want an answer that critically analyzes a topic, you could include instructions like "Critically analyze..." in your prompt.

Repeat and refine

Prompt engineering is an iterative process. Sometimes, you won't get exactly what you want the first time. That's where repetition and refinement come in. Modify your prompt, experiment with different approaches, and learn from each trial. Over time, you'll become more adept at formulating prompts that deliver the desired results.

Managing limits

Even though language models like ChatGPT are incredibly powerful, they still have their limits. Sometimes, a prompt can be too complex or ambiguous to get a good response. In these cases, it can be useful to split your prompt into several simpler questions, or to provide more context to help the AI understand what you want.

Stay open to surprises

One of the most fascinating aspects of language patterns is their ability to surprise and inspire. Even if you have a specific goal in mind, remain open to the unexpected. You may be surprised by the creativity, insight or humor that AI can generate.

Ultimately, prompt engineering transcends simple human-computer interaction. It represents the intersection of art and science, since it requires both a technical understanding of the functionalities of a language model and a creative sensibility for developing prompts that will generate the desired responses.

It's a process of continuous experimentation and learning. Every interaction with a language model is an opportunity to learn and adjust your approach. Prompts that work well can be refined for even better performance, and those that don't deliver the desired results can be revised or rethought. This constant iteration is fundamental to mastering the art of prompt engineering.

Learning doesn't stop there. As language models evolve and become more powerful, new opportunities and challenges arise. Formulating effective prompts requires constant adaptation to these evolutions, which makes this field both stimulating and rewarding.

With these tips and tricks, your ability to formulate prompts can improve significantly. Not only will you be able to make the most of language models like ChatGPT, but you'll also be able to enrich your understanding of the potential of conversational AI.

Whether for professional, educational or creative applications, or simply for the personal satisfaction of an engaging conversation with an AI, effective mastery of prompt engineering will open up new horizons for you. So it's important to keep exploring, learning and innovating in this exciting field.

-15-

Maximize your results

"Artificial intelligence will help us become a better version of ourselves."

Rana el Kaliouby

Advances in artificial intelligence have made impressive leaps in recent years, leading to a profound transformation in the way we interact with technology. At the heart of this revolution are language models like ChatGPT, which have enabled new forms of dialogue and collaboration between man and machine. However, to make the most of these powerful tools, it's necessary to master the subtle art of formulating prompts.

The ability to design professional prompts for ChatGPT involves more than simply transmitting a query to a computer system. It requires a high degree of precision, clarity and context to guide the language model towards the production of relevant, high-quality results. Whether it's to gain an illuminating insight into a complex subject, generate a detailed answer to a specific question or even create creative content, the art of formulating prompts is a major skill for any effective interaction with this incredible tool.

In the following sections, we'll take a deep dive into the process of formulating prompts, exploring the techniques and strategies that achieve the best results from ChatGPT. We'll discuss the importance of clarity and specificity, how to provide appropriate context to guide AI responses, the usefulness of specifying the desired response format, and the strategic use of commands to control AI behavior.

Beyond theory, we'll also look at practical examples and case studies that illustrate these concepts in action. Through the exploration of prompts that have led to impressive results, we'll demonstrate how these principles can be effectively applied in a variety of scenarios.

Whether you're a technology professional looking to maximize the effectiveness of your interactions with AI, or simply curious to understand how these language models work, this guide is designed to equip you with the tools and knowledge you need to formulate prompts professionally. So get ready to embark on an exciting journey through the art and science of prompter engineering, where every word counts and every detail can make a difference.

The Art of Formulating a Professional Prompt

A well-formulated prompt is the first step towards successful interaction with ChatGPT. This essential skill requires an understanding of language structure, appropriate context and the precision needed to guide the artificial intelligence to an effective response. In this chapter, we'll break down these key elements to understand how to professionally formulate a prompt that drives ChatGPT to deliver impressive results.

Clarity and specificity

The first rule when formulating a prompt for this conversational model is to be clear and precise. Avoid ambiguity or vague wording that could lead to multiple interpretations. The more precise you are in your query, the more relevant and useful the generated response will be. For example, instead of asking "What are the new technologies?", be more specific by asking "What are the new technologies for sustainable development in 2023?

Contextualization

Context is essential when formulating prompts. For best results, give the AI as much detail as possible to frame your request. For example, if you want this tool to write an article on the circular economy, you could start with: "Write a 500-word article on the circular economy, explaining its importance for environmental sustainability and citing examples of companies adopting this model."

Answer format

Don't hesitate to tell ChatGPT what format you'd like the answer to be in. Would you like a list? A detailed paragraph? A series of questions and answers? For example, if you want a list of ideas for a project, you could say: "List five innovative ideas for a sustainable development project in the energy sector".

Using Commands

Finally, don't forget that you can use commands to guide the AI's behavior. For example, by adding "-ia" to the end of your prompt, you can tell ChatGPT that you expect a more detailed response.

By mastering these key elements, you'll be able to formulate effective prompts that accurately guide the model, delivering high-quality results that meet your needs. In the next chapter, we'll explore concrete examples and case studies to illustrate these concepts in action.

Use Prompts to achieve impressive results

Having gained a basic understanding of how prompts are formulated in the first chapter, it's time to dive into some real-life examples to see these principles in action. Let's take a look at a few prompts that have produced remarkable and relevant results.

Creativity request: "Create a short romantic poem that uses the metaphor of the moon and stars."

In this prompt, we give a precise context (romantic poem), a specific subject (metaphor of the moon and stars), and the format (short poem). ChatGPT then has all the information it needs to generate an appropriate response.

Content Writing: "Write a press release for the announcement of a new sustainable technology product, with details of its features, environmental benefits and launch date."

Here, we ask for a specific format (press release), with particular elements to be included (features, environmental benefits, launch date). This guides OpenAI's conversational model towards a detailed and relevant response.

Consultation on Ideas: "Proposes five ideas for improving employee engagement in a remote company, with a focus on communication and well-being."

In this prompt, we explicitly ask for a number of ideas (five), focused on a particular theme (employee engagement), with sub-themes (communication, well-being).

Learning Need: "Explains Einstein's principle of relativity using simple terms and everyday examples."

For this prompt, we ask for an explanation of a complex subject, but using simple language and concrete examples. This guides this conversational model to provide an accessible and understandable response.

Brainstorm: "Generate a list of ten potential names for a mobile fitness app that focuses on meditation and yoga."

By specifying the number (ten), the type of suggestions (mobile app names), and the subject (meditation and yoga), we guide ChatGPT towards a creative and targeted response.

These examples illustrate how the use of precise, detailed prompts can guide ChatGPT to achieve incredible results. In the next chapter, we'll look at common mistakes to avoid when formulating prompts and how to improve prompts for even better results.

Common mistakes to avoid and how to improve Prompts

Mastering the formulation of prompts for ChatGPT is a skill that may take a little time and experience to develop fully. However, knowing some common mistakes can help you avoid them and improve your prompts faster. Here are some common mistakes to avoid:

Lack of precision: As mentioned earlier, one of the most common mistakes is not being specific enough. Vague or general prompts can lead to equally vague responses. Be as specific as possible to get the most relevant results.

Omission of context: Omitting necessary context can lead to irrelevant or inappropriate responses. Providing clear, relevant context can help guide the AI's response.

Don't define the format: if you have a specific format in mind for the answer, make sure you specify it in your prompt. Otherwise, the AI may choose a format that doesn't match your expectations.

Excessive use of jargon: Although ChatGPT can understand a wide range of terms and concepts, excessive use of jargon or technical terms can sometimes lead to errors or misunderstandings. Try to keep your prompts clear and understandable.

Now that we've covered what to avoid, here are a few tips for improving your prompts:

Experiment: feel free to test different types of prompts to see how the AI reacts. This can help you understand how to formulate your prompts more effectively.

Review and adjust: if the AI's response doesn't meet your expectations, review your prompt and try again. Sometimes a slight adjustment can make all the difference.

Use commands: don't forget that you can use commands to guide the AI's behavior. For example, by adding "-ia" to the end of your prompt, you can tell ChatGPT that you expect a more detailed response.

Stay up to date: like all technology, this conversational model is constantly evolving. Stay up to date with the latest features and enhancements to get the most out of this technology.

By avoiding these common mistakes and following these tips, you can formulate prompts more effectively to achieve even better results with AI. In the next chapter, we'll explore how to use ChatGPT for specific applications and look at a few case studies.

Specific ChatGPT applications and case studies

ChatGPT can be used in a multitude of scenarios. Its ability to generate coherent text and understand context makes it valuable in a variety of fields. In this chapter, we'll explore how to use ChatGPT for specific applications and look at a few case studies.

Creative content

ChatGPT can be used to generate creative content. Whether writing stories, poems, or even scripts for plays or films, this template can help stimulate creativity and provide a basis for creative work.

For example, a writer might give the following prompt: "Create a plot for a science fiction thriller set in a future where mankind can travel through time." The result could serve as a starting point for the development of a novel or screenplay.

Editorial assistance

ChatGPT can also help with more formal texts, such as blog posts, speeches, cover letters, and even academic papers. A student might, for example, ask, "Write a one-page summary of the impact of the Industrial Revolution on modern society."

Learning and teaching

This tool can be used as a teaching aid. It can explain complex concepts in a simple way, provide information on a variety of topics, and even help with revision. An example prompt might be, "Explains the Pythagorean theorem in a simple way for a ten-year-old."

Idea generation and brainstorming

This model is also useful for generating ideas. Whether for a new product, a business project, or to solve a complex problem, ChatGPT can provide a variety of ideas and perspectives. For example, an entrepreneur might ask, "Give five ideas for a technological product that could help reduce the environmental impact of households."

Customer care

Finally, ChatGPT can be used as a customer support tool. It can answer questions, provide information about products or services, and help solve problems. A company could use ChatGPT to answer common customer questions, giving prompts such as, "Explains how to configure our product X for a new user."

Each specific application requires an appropriate prompt formulation to achieve the best results. By understanding how ChatGPT works and how it responds to prompts, you can optimize your applications for accurate, helpful and creative responses. In the next chapter, we'll go even deeper and explore advanced strategies for maximizing the effectiveness of your prompts.

Strategies for maximizing the efficiency of Prompts

Having explored prompt formulation, mistakes to avoid, possible improvements and specific applications of ChatGPT, it's time to delve deeper and discover advanced strategies for maximizing the effectiveness of your prompts. Here are a few strategies to consider:

Using language modifiers

ChatGPT is sensitive to the language you use. For example, the tone, level of formality and clarity of the prompt can influence the response. For a more formal response, you might say: "Could you explain... ?" For a less formal response, you might use: "Can you tell me...?"

Prompts sequencing

Sometimes, a complex question can be better handled by breaking it down into several simpler prompts. For example, instead of asking "What is behavioral economics and how is it used in marketing?" you could first ask "What is behavioral economics?" and then "How is behavioral economics used in marketing?"

Unexpected Response Management

If this conversational model produces an unexpected response, it may be useful to rephrase your prompt or add more details to clarify your request. For example, if you ask "How does the brain work?", and the answer is too general, you can rephrase by asking "Can you explain how the brain processes sensory information?"

Using Multi-phase Prompts

For more complex questions, you can guide ChatGPT through several steps to get a more detailed answer. For example, if you want to know how to start a business, you might first ask "What are the first steps to starting a business?", then "What are the legal considerations when starting a business?", and finally "What are some tips for succeeding as a new entrepreneur?"

Exploring different models

Don't forget that there are several versions of this model, each with different capabilities and specialties. For example, larger models may be better at generating creative and detailed responses, while smaller models may be faster and more efficient for simpler tasks.

By adopting these advanced strategies, you can get the most out of ChatGPT, improving the accuracy, relevance and quality of its responses. In the final chapter, we'll recap everything we've learned and explore how to continue learning and growing with this incredible technology.

Summary

In previous chapters, we've explored in depth the art and science of formulating prompts for ChatGPT. We've discovered how to create effective prompts, how to avoid common mistakes, how to improve our prompts and how to use this tool for a variety of specific applications. We also explored advanced strategies for maximizing the effectiveness of our prompts. So, where do we go from here?

The world of artificial intelligence is constantly evolving, and ChatGPT is no exception. As the technology continues to advance, new features and capabilities will undoubtedly be added, offering even more possibilities for use. It's important to keep up to date with these developments to get the most out of ChatGPT.

Practice is the best way to improve your prompter skills. Don't hesitate to experiment, test different types of prompts and learn from your mistakes. Every interaction with this tool is an opportunity to learn and improve.

It's also useful to share your experiences and learnings with others. Whether by joining online forums, participating in discussion groups, or sharing your own tips and tricks, exchanging information and ideas can be very beneficial.

Finally, don't forget to keep an open and curious mind. ChatGPT is an incredibly powerful tool, but it's also a fascinating technology that gives us a glimpse of what the future of AI might hold. Take the time to explore, marvel and appreciate all that this conversational model has to offer.

In short, using ChatGPT effectively is a skill that can be learned and honed over time. With practice, patience, and a constant willingness to learn and grow, you can maximize the potential of this technology to achieve your goals, whether that's generating creative content, solving complex problems, answering questions, or simply exploring the fascinating possibilities of artificial intelligence. So keep experimenting, keep learning, and above all, have fun!

Here are a few tips to help you on your way:

Understanding language models: language models, like GPT, are based on deep neural network architectures. A good understanding of the fundamentals of machine learning, deep learning and neural networks can help you better understand how these models generate answers.

Practice writing prompts: Like any skill, writing effective prompts improves with practice. Experiment with different types of prompts, try out different approaches, and learn from your mistakes.

Familiarize yourself with ChatGPT: use ChatGPT as much as possible to understand its strengths and weaknesses. This will help you understand how to formulate prompts that get the best results.

Be creative: The best prompts often come from creative thinking. Don't just follow predefined formulas; try out new ideas and approaches.

Learn from the community: There are many online resources, from forums to blogs, where you can learn from the experience of others, get ideas for prompts, and ask questions.

Keep abreast of developments in AI and ML: the field of artificial intelligence and ML is evolving rapidly. Stay up to date on the latest research, new model architectures, and best practices.

Apply your skills to real projects: nothing beats hands-on experience. Try applying your skills to real projects, whether it's creating your own chat bot, generating content for a blog, or helping a company improve its customer service with ChatGPT.

Be analytical: evaluate the responses you get from your prompts. What went well? What could have been improved? This analysis can help you hone your prompter skills.

Adapt to user needs: if you're working on applications for end-users, understand their needs and expectations. This will help you formulate prompts that provide useful and relevant answers.

-16-

Exercises for training and improvement

"Creativity is the secret of AI. It's our ability to create and innovate that will make the difference between man and machine."

Hassabis Demis

Artificial intelligence, and more specifically language models like ChatGPT, have opened new doors in the field of technology. They have the potential to transform the way we work, learn and communicate. However, to fully exploit this potential, it is essential to understand how to interact effectively with these models. That's where prompts come in.

Prompts are the instructions or questions we give the AI to guide its response. Writing effective prompts is an art in itself, requiring both a technical understanding of how language models work and a touch of creativity to come up with questions that will elicit useful and interesting responses.

To help you develop your prompts skills, we've designed a series of exercises of increasing difficulty. These exercises will guide you through a variety of scenarios, allowing you to explore the different ways in which you can use prompts to interact with AI.

The first exercises start with basic concepts, helping you to understand how simple prompts can be used to elicit direct responses from artificial intelligence. As you progress, the exercises become more complex, inviting you to write prompts that guide not only the content of the AI's response, but also its form, tone and style.

Intermediate exercises encourage you to experiment with more nuanced and contextual prompts, iterate and revise your prompts, and use prompts to stimulate learning, creativity and reflection. You'll also begin to explore how prompts can be used to simulate specific situations, characters and voices.

Finally, the most advanced exercises challenge you to push the limits of what AI can do. You'll be invited to write prompts that ask artificial intelligence to generate complex scenarios, solve problems, make predictions, ponder deep philosophical questions, and more. These exercises will help you understand the limits and possibilities of AI, and develop advanced prompt writing skills.

This series of exercises is designed to help you become a master prompter, able to interact effectively with language patterns to get the answers you want. So get ready to explore, experiment and learn. Good luck!

Exercise 1: Warming up with simple Prompts

Start with simple prompts that require a direct response from the AI. For example, "What is photosynthesis?" or "Who wrote 'Les Misérables'?". Note how the AI responds directly to your questions and use these examples to better understand how simple prompts work.

Exercise 2: Creating complex Prompts

Once you're comfortable with simple prompts, try creating more complex ones. For example, instead of simply asking "What is photosynthesis?", you could ask "Explain photosynthesis to a 5-year-old child". This forces the AI to think harder and formulate an answer tailored to the target audience.

Exercise 3: Guidance on response form

Try writing prompts that guide not only the content of the answer, but also its form. For example, you could ask: "Can you write a short poem about photosynthesis?". This shows how prompts can be used to direct AI towards specific types of response.

Exercise 4: Specific and contextualized Prompts

Use your prompts to give artificial intelligence more context. For example, you might ask: "As a biologist specializing in botany, can you explain photosynthesis to a first-year biology student?". Here, context gives the AI additional information to adapt its answer.

Exercise 5: Iterating and revising Prompts

This exercise will help you understand the importance of iteration in writing prompts. Take a prompt you've written previously that didn't produce the results you expected. Think about how you could modify it to get a better response. Try several variations and note the differences in the AI's responses.

Exercise 6: Learning Prompts

Try using prompts to learn something new. For example, you could ask, "Can you give me a detailed introduction to the history of contemporary art?". Use this exercise to explore how prompts can be used for learning and education.

Exercise 7: Natural language commands

Explore the possibilities of getting specific answers using natural language commands. For example, instead of simply asking "What is AI?", try phrasing your prompt as a command: "Give me a summary of artificial intelligence suitable for a non-technical audience".

Exercise 8: Simulation Prompts

This exercise involves using prompts to simulate situations or characters. For example, you could write: "Imagine you're Shakespeare and write a sonnet about artificial intelligence". This can help develop your creativity and see how AI can adapt to different voices and styles.

Exercise 9: Prompts for reflection

Use your prompts to stimulate deep or philosophical thinking. For example, "What might be the ethical implications of AI in the future?". These types of prompts can help generate interesting and thought-provoking discussions.

Exercise 10: Feedback and improvement

This exercise focuses on learning from AI responses. After receiving a response to a prompt, take a moment to think about how you could improve the prompt to get a better response. This might involve making the prompt more specific, changing the tone, or adding more context.

Exercise 11: Prompts for creative inspiration

Turn to AI for creative inspiration. For example, "Give me an original idea for a science fiction short story". This type of prompt can be very useful for stimulating creativity and innovation.

Exercise 12: Exploration Prompts

Don't be afraid to explore the limits of what AI can do. You can try to create prompts that involve complex topics or that require the AI to generate creative or innovative content. Remember, the goal is to understand what AI can and can't do, and learn how to formulate your prompts accordingly.

Exercise 13: Narrative Prompts

Ask the artificial intelligence to tell a story based on specific parameters. For example, "Tell a science fiction story set on Mars in the future". This will help you understand how AI can generate coherent, engaging narratives.

Exercise 14: Debate prompts

Try creating a prompt that invites AI to present both sides of an argument. For example, "What are the pros and cons of AI in education?". This can help you understand how AI can handle complex, nuanced topics.

Exercise 15: Writing style tips

Ask the AI to write in a specific style. For example, "Write a paragraph on photosynthesis in the style of J.K. Rowling". This can help you understand how artificial intelligence can adapt its writing style.

Exercise 16: Problem-solving Prompts

Use prompts to ask the AI to solve a problem. For example, "How could I reduce my energy consumption at home?". This can help you understand how AI can come up with practical solutions.

Exercise 17: Prediction Prompts

Ask the AI to make a prediction based on certain information. For example, "What could be the major technological trends in the next 10 years?". This can help you understand how AI can anticipate future trends or events.

Exercise 18: Rapid idea generation

Ask the AI to generate ideas for a project or task. For example, "What are some ideas for a science project on the theme of ecology?". This can help you understand how artificial intelligence can stimulate creativity and innovation.

Exercise 19: Clarification Prompts

Ask the artificial intelligence to clarify a complex idea or concept. For example, "Can you explain the theory of relativity as if I had no knowledge of physics?". This can help you understand how AI can simplify complex concepts.

Exercise 20: Role simulation Prompts

Ask the AI to simulate a specific role. For example, "Imagine you're a tour guide in Paris. What would you recommend I visit?". This can help you understand how artificial intelligence can adapt to different roles and contexts.

Exercise 21: Prompts for personal reflection

Ask the artificial intelligence to think about a personal question. For example, "If you were human, what would be your favorite hobby?". This can help you understand how AI can generate introspective answers.

Exercise 22: Question generation prompts

Ask the AI to generate questions on a specific topic. For example, "What questions might I ask in an interview with an astronaut?". This can help you understand how artificial intelligence can help prepare interviews or discussions.

Exercise 23: Text revision prompts

Give the AI a paragraph of text and ask them to revise or improve it. For example, "Here's a paragraph from my essay. Can you make it more persuasive?". This can help you understand how AI can help improve writing.

Exercise 24: Prompts for generating securities

Ask the AI to generate a title for an article, book or film based on a brief description. For example, "What would be a good title for a science fiction book about a human colony on Mars?". This can help you understand how artificial intelligence can help create catchy titles.

Exercise 25: Prompts for scenario generation

Ask the AI to generate a complex scenario. For example, "Create a detailed scenario for a science fiction film set in a post-apocalyptic future". This can help you understand how AI can develop complex, detailed ideas.

Exercise 26: Logical deduction Prompts

Ask a question that requires logical deduction on the part of the AI. For example, "If all A's are B's, and all B's are C's, are all A's C's?". This can help you understand how artificial intelligence handles logic.

Exercise 27: Metaphor generation Prompts

Ask the AI to generate a metaphor for a complex concept. For example, "Can you create a metaphor to explain quantum theory?". This can help you understand how artificial intelligence can use creative images to explain complex ideas.

Exercise 28: Literary criticism tips

Ask the artificial intelligence to analyze and criticize a literary passage. For example, "What is your analysis of this passage from 'Moby Dick'?". This can help you understand how AI can interpret and criticize literature.

Exercise 29: Advanced problem solvers

Pose a complex problem to the AI and ask it to propose a solution. For example, "How could we solve the problem of climate change?". This can help you understand how artificial intelligence can tackle large-scale problems.

Exercise 30: Trend prediction prompts

Ask the AI to predict a future trend in a specific field based on current information. For example, "What might be the future trends in artificial intelligence technology?". This can help you understand how AI can anticipate future developments.

Exercise 31: Theory generation prompts

Ask the AI to generate a theory on a given topic. For example, "What could be a theory about the origin of the universe?". This can help you understand how AI can generate theoretical ideas.

Exercise 32: Prompts for simulating conversations

Ask the AI to simulate a conversation between two or more characters. For example, "Simulate a conversation between Albert Einstein and Isaac Newton about the nature of gravity". This can help you understand how artificial intelligence can handle complex interactions.

Exercise 33: Advanced poetry generation prompts

Ask the artificial intelligence to generate a complex poem with specific constraints. For example, "Write a sonnet in iambic pentameter on the theme of lost love". This can help you understand how AI can create poetry with specific constraints.

Exercise 34: Prompts for generating word games

Ask the artificial intelligence to generate a pun or joke. For example, "Can you create an astronomy-themed pun?". This can help you understand how AI can use humor and wordplay.

Exercise 35: Prompts for generating hypothetical scenarios

Ask the AI to generate a scenario based on a hypothetical situation. For example, "What would happen if the dinosaurs had never disappeared?". This can help you understand how artificial intelligence can explore hypothetical scenarios.

Exercise 36: Philosophy generation prompts

Ask the AI to generate a philosophical reflection on a given topic. For example, "What are your thoughts on the concept of free will?". This can help you understand how AI can address deep philosophical questions.

Exercise 37: Speech generation prompts

Ask the AI to generate a speech on a complex and controversial topic, such as the ethics of artificial intelligence. For example, "Write a persuasive speech on the importance of ethics in the development of AI". This can help you understand how artificial intelligence can structure a coherent and persuasive argument on a complex topic, while taking into account different perspectives and issues.

Exercise 38: Prompt generation of futuristic scenarios

Ask the AI to generate a futuristic scenario based on current technological trends. For example, "Imagine a scenario where AI has completely transformed the way we live and work in 2050". This can help you understand how AI can extrapolate current trends to imagine possible futures, while taking into account social, economic and ethical implications.

Exercise 39: Prompts for generating advanced scientific concepts

Ask the AI to generate an explanation of an advanced scientific concept, such as string theory. For example, "Can you explain string theory to someone with no background in physics?". This can help you understand how AI can simplify and communicate complex scientific concepts in an accessible way.

Exercise 40: Art review generation speeds

Ask the AI to generate a review of a work of art based on a detailed description. For example, "Here's a detailed description of a painting by Van Gogh. Can you provide an analysis and critique of this work?". This can help you understand how AI can interpret and evaluate art from text descriptions.

Exercise 41: Prompts for generating corporate strategies

Ask the AI to generate a business strategy for a specific scenario. For example, "Imagine you're the CEO of a fast-growing tech start-up. What would be your strategy for managing increased competition in the market?". This can help you understand how artificial intelligence can analyze business situations and propose viable strategies.

Exercise 42: Prompts for generating conflict resolution scenarios

Ask the artificial intelligence to generate a conflict resolution scenario. For example, "Imagine a conflict between two colleagues at work. How could you resolve this conflict fairly and effectively?". This can help you understand how AI can propose conflict resolution solutions that take into account the perspectives and feelings of all parties involved.

Exercise 43: Prompts for generating science fiction scenarios

Ask the AI to generate a complex and detailed science fiction scenario. For example, "Create a scenario for a science fiction novel that explores the implications of the discovery of intelligent extraterrestrial life". This can help you understand how AI can imagine futuristic scenarios that explore deep and challenging themes.

Exercise 44: Philosophy of mind generation prompts

Ask the AI to generate a reflection on a complex concept in philosophy of mind, such as consciousness. For example, "What is your reflection on the nature of consciousness and how it relates to artificial intelligence?". This can help you understand how artificial intelligence can address deep and complex philosophical questions.

Exercise 45: Prompts for generating sustainable development scenarios

Ask the AI to generate a scenario about how we might achieve sustainable development on a global scale. For example, "Imagine a scenario where the world managed to achieve the United Nations Sustainable Development Goals by 2030". This can help you understand how AI can envision solutions to complex global challenges.

Exercise 46: Prompts for generating global problem-solving scenarios

Ask the artificial intelligence to generate a scenario about how we might solve a major global problem, such as world hunger. For example, "Imagine a scenario where the world has successfully eradicated hunger by 2030". This can help you understand how AI can envision solutions to complex global problems.

Exercise 47: Prompts for generating global policy scenarios

Ask the artificial intelligence to generate a scenario about a world political event. For example, "Imagine a scenario where tensions between major world powers have been resolved peacefully". This can help you understand how AI can envision solutions to global political challenges.

Exercise 48: Emerging technology scenario generation prompts

Ask the AI to generate a scenario about an emerging technology, such as nuclear fusion. For example, "Imagine a scenario where nuclear fusion has become a viable and widely used energy source." This can help you understand how AI can envision the potential impact of emerging technologies.

Exercise 49: Prompts for generating scenarios of social change

Ask the artificial intelligence to generate a scenario about a major social change. For example, "Imagine a scenario where gender equality has been fully achieved on a global scale". This can help you understand how AI can envision solutions to complex social challenges.

Exercise 50: Generating scenarios for a scientific revolution

Ask the AI to generate a scenario about a major scientific revolution. For example, "Imagine a scenario where we discovered definitive proof of the multiverse theory". This can help you understand how artificial intelligence can consider the implications of major scientific discoveries.

Congratulations on completing this series of prompt writing exercises! You've explored a range of scenarios, techniques and challenges, and gained a deeper understanding of how language models like ChatGPT can be guided to produce useful, creative and relevant responses.

During these exercises, you learned how to formulate simple and complex prompts, guide the form and tone of responses, give AI context, iterate and revise your prompts, and use prompts to stimulate learning, creativity and reflection. You also explored how prompts can be used to simulate specific situations, characters and voices, and were challenged to push the boundaries of what artificial intelligence can do.

These skills will prove invaluable as you continue to interact with language models in your work, study or leisure. Whether you're using AI to help write texts, generate creative ideas, learn new topics, or explore complex scenarios, you're now better equipped to guide artificial intelligence effectively.

However, remember that learning is a continuous process. Language models and artificial intelligence in general are evolving rapidly, and there will always be new techniques to learn, new challenges to overcome, and new possibilities to explore. Feel free to return to these exercises from time to time to refresh your skills, or seek out other resources to continue deepening your understanding.

Finally, don't forget that the ultimate goal of writing prompts is to facilitate effective and rewarding interaction with AI. So keep experimenting, get creative and have fun with your prompts. You'll be amazed at what you and AI can achieve together. Good luck on your learning journey with AI !

-17-

Bonus

"AI is the future, and the future is here now."

Bill Gates

50 prompts to get your business off the ground:

Develop a business model for a platform that connects local artisans to global markets, using AI technology to predict trends, optimize pricing and streamline logistics.

Imagine a service that uses drones for last-mile delivery of fresh, local produce. Describe the operational process, customer benefits and potential challenges of this venture.

Offer a virtual reality platform that provides immersive travel experiences for people who can't physically travel due to financial, health or time constraints.

Consider a subscription service for personalized learning experiences, where AI matches users with tailored educational content based on their interests, learning style and career goals.

Create a business plan for a technology-driven personal health consulting service using AI to analyze health data and provide personalized advice on diet, exercise and stress management.

Design a marketplace for renting and sharing seldom-used household items to promote a circular economy, reduce waste and foster community ties.

Offer a micro-investment platform enabling individuals to invest small sums of money in small businesses or local start-ups.

Develop a business model for a smart home service that uses AI to optimize energy consumption, automate routine tasks and enhance home security.

Create a plan for a coworking space that also offers childcare services, meeting the needs of entrepreneurial parents.

Imagine a software solution that uses AI to help companies identify sustainable practices relevant to their industry, calculate their carbon footprint and track their progress towards achieving their environmental goals.

Develop a platform that uses machine learning to connect freelance creatives with clients looking for specific styles or aesthetics. This platform could cover a wide range of creative professions, such as graphic design, writing, music and art.

Propose a company that creates customizable 3D-printed prostheses, using AI to ensure a perfect fit and personalized design.

Consider a personalized nutrition service that uses AI to analyze dietary needs and food preferences, then delivers customized meal plans and ingredients to the customer's door.

Create a business plan for a carbon offset service that allows individuals and companies to invest in renewable energy projects, reforestation efforts and other environmentally friendly initiatives.

Design an AI-driven tutoring service that identifies a student's weaknesses and tailors lessons to strengthen those areas, while reinforcing their strengths.

Develop a virtual assistant service specifically for small businesses, providing administrative, financial and customer support through AI.

Offer a platform that uses AI to provide real-time translation services, bridging language gaps during business meetings, conferences and social interactions.

Imagine a company that integrates IoT and AI to optimize urban farming practices, increasing efficiency and yield in limited spaces.

Create a business model for an AI-driven mental health platform that connects users with certified therapists and offers personalized mental wellness resources.

Design a local recycling service that uses AI to sort materials, improve efficiency and maximize the value extracted from waste.

Develop a company that uses augmented reality (AR) to provide real estate agencies with virtual home staging services, enabling potential buyers to visualize different furniture and decorating options.

To offer a peer-to-peer lending platform specifically designed to finance renewable energy projects, such as the installation of solar panels and wind farms.

Imagine a company offering personalized fitness programs based on genetic and biometric data, with AI analyzing each customer's unique needs.

Create a service that uses AI to automate and optimize the management of personal finances, including investments, budgeting and savings.

Develop a platform that connects consumers with sustainable local farmers, supporting the local economy and providing access to fresh, organic produce.

Consider a company that uses AI to provide personalized recommendations for experiences in local areas, such as an AI concierge for exploring neighborhoods.

Suggest a company that offers waste-to-energy solutions for small businesses, turning organic waste into biofuel or compost.

Imagine an e-learning platform that uses AI to adapt course material to the learner's pace and understanding, making e-learning more effective and personalized.

Develop a business model for an online platform enabling users to rent their appliances or tools, to encourage the sharing economy and reduce overall consumption.

Create a smart product rental service for businesses, providing on-demand items such as projectors, sound equipment or even vehicles, reducing the need for companies to purchase and maintain these assets.

Design an AI-powered platform that helps users create personalized skincare routines based on their unique skin characteristics, lifestyle and environmental factors.

Propose a business idea for a network of co-location spaces optimized for remote workers and digital nomads, with high-speed Internet, comfortable workspaces and community-building activities.

Imagine a subscription service that offers bespoke boxes of second-hand clothing, selected according to the customer's style preferences, size and season. This service supports fashion's circular economy and promotes sustainable consumption habits.

Develop a platform that uses AI to detect and report online privacy breaches, giving individuals and businesses greater control over their digital information.

Create a business model for an eco-friendly meal kit delivery service, sourcing local ingredients and offering plant-based options.

Consider a pet-sitting service that uses AI to match pet owners with sitters who have experience with specific breeds and needs.

To propose a company that provides environmentally friendly, modular tiny homes for affordable housing solutions, using a direct-to-consumer model.

Develop a platform to connect socially responsible companies with consumers who value sustainability, in order to promote ethical consumption.

Imagine a company that creates immersive virtual reality experiences for remote team-building, offering a unique solution to companies with dispersed employees.

Designing a concierge service for the elderly that uses AI to monitor health, schedule appointments, manage medication and offer companionship, to improve the quality of life of older people living independently.

Offer a service that uses AI to analyze a user's digital footprint and help them build a positive, authentic image online. This service could be particularly useful for professionals and small businesses.

Design a subscription box for learning new skills, such as coding, cooking, painting, etc.

Imagine a company using blockchain technology to create a transparent and fair platform for independent musicians to distribute their music and receive fair remuneration.

Create a business model for a gamified fitness app that connects to various exercise equipment and wearables, fostering a virtual fitness community and promoting healthy competition.

Consider an app that uses AI to recommend sustainable and ethical alternatives for everyday products, to make it easier for consumers to make considered purchasing decisions.

Develop a virtual interior design service that uses AR and AI to help users visualize changes to their living spaces in real time, providing personalized recommendations based on style preferences and budget.

Propose a company that uses AI to provide dynamic pricing for services such as energy, parking or public transport, adjusting prices based on demand, time or other relevant factors.

Create a digital platform that connects mentors and mentees in various industries around the world, to promote knowledge sharing and professional development.

Imagine a technology-based concierge service for tourists that uses AI to recommend experiences based on personal preferences, local trends and real-time data such as weather and crowds.

To develop a company that manufactures customizable, eco-friendly modular furniture that can be adapted to different spaces and uses over time, reducing waste and promoting sustainable living.

Take action, make these potential projects a reality for yourself, and improve your future with the help of **AI**. You won't be alone in this adventure, and you'll benefit from invaluable, evolving help.

The 50 Prompts to discover the potential of AI :

Design a fictional world with its own ecosystem, cultures and technologies. What are the key elements of this world, and how do its inhabitants interact with each other?

Imagine you could merge the abilities of two animals to create a new super-creature. Which animals would you choose, and what would be the characteristics of the new creature? What impact would it have on the world?

If you were to create a new universal language from scratch, what would its main features be? Describe its phonetic system, grammar, writing system and any unique linguistic features.

Write a story in which humans discover that the universe is actually a computer simulation and find a way to "hack" it to their advantage. What do they do, and what are the consequences?

Describe a utopian society based on the principles of sustainable living and radical empathy. What would its political system, economy, education and social structure look like?

Invent a new form of entertainment that combines elements of different art forms (e.g. music, visual arts, literature and theater). Explain the rules or guidelines of this new art form and describe a performance.

Imagine a world where emotions are traded like commodities. How would this affect interpersonal relationships, and what would be the potential implications for society as a whole?

Write an alternative history in which a vanished civilization has survived and prospered to the present day. Describe their culture, their achievements and how they have influenced the modern world.

Propose a solution to one of humanity's greatest challenges (e.g. climate change, income inequality or global health) using a cutting-edge technology that doesn't yet exist. Describe how this new technology would work and the impact it would have on society.

Write a dialogue between two self-aware artificial intelligences discussing the nature of their existence, their purpose and their relationship with humans.

Imagine a world where people can exchange their talents and skills. Describe the process of exchanging these capabilities and how it would affect society, work and personal relationships.

Write a story in which a person wakes up one day with the ability to see into parallel universes. Describe his experiences, the differences he observes and how this new power changes his life.

Create a new sport that can be played both on Earth and in weightless environments, such as the International Space Station. Describe the sport's rules, equipment and strategies.

Imagine a future where emotions can be transmitted and felt through virtual reality. How would this technology affect human interaction, mental health and the way we process emotions?

Write a letter from an extraterrestrial being who has been observing Earth for centuries, detailing his observations, opinions and advice to mankind.

Imagine a society where people can live indefinitely by transferring their consciousness into new bodies. Describe the implications of this technology on population, ethics and personal identity.

Create a new mythology for a fictional culture, complete with gods, heroes and supernatural creatures. Describe the key stories, rituals and beliefs that shape this mythology.

Write a story set in a world where humans have discovered how to communicate with animals. Explore the new relationships developing between different species and how this ability is changing society.

Propose a futuristic transportation system that could revolutionize the way people get around. Explain the technology behind it, its impact on the environment and how it would reshape cities and landscapes.

Write a conversation between a time traveler from the distant future and a historical figure from the past. Describe the exchange of ideas, perspectives and the impact of this encounter on both characters.

Imagine a society where dreams can be recorded and shared like movies. Describe the impact of this technology on entertainment, relationships and privacy.

Write a story set in a world where every human being is born with a unique superpower. Explore how this power shapes the lives of individuals, society and the balance of power between nations.

Create a fictional culinary tradition with unique dishes, ingredients and cooking techniques. Describe the flavors, textures and cultural significance of this cuisine.

Imagine a future where artificial intelligence and robots have replaced most jobs. Describe how humans spend their time, the new forms of work that emerge and the challenges that arise.

Write a letter from an advanced civilization in a distant galaxy, which has observed Earth and wishes to make contact with it. Describe their culture, technology and intentions towards humanity.

Propose a new type of education system that better prepares individuals for the challenges and opportunities of the future. Describe the curriculum, teaching methods and learning environments of this new system.

Write a story in which a person discovers that he or she can manipulate the fabric of reality by altering the laws of physics. Explore the consequences and ethical dilemmas of possessing such power.

Imagine a world where people can download and install new knowledge and skills directly into their brains. Describe the implications for learning, work and society as a whole.

Create a detailed map of an imaginary city, complete with neighborhoods, landmarks and public spaces. Describe the history, culture and daily life of the city's inhabitants.

Write a dialogue between a human and an advanced AI who debate the pros and cons of merging human consciousness and artificial intelligence, exploring the potential benefits and risks.

Imagine a world where people can instantly change their appearance at will. Describe the impact of this ability on fashion, relationships and personal identity.

Write a story about a lost civilization hidden deep beneath the Earth's surface. Describe the journey to discover this underground world, its inhabitants and their unique way of life.

Create a new musical genre that fuses elements of different existing styles. Describe the characteristics of this new genre, its instrumentation and the emotions it arouses in listeners.

Imagine a future where humans have colonized planets all over the galaxy. Describe the challenges faced by these interstellar colonists and the various societies they have created.

Write a conversation between a person and his or her own consciousness, which has manifested as a separate entity. Explore the dialogue between the two people as they discuss the person's actions, choices and beliefs.

Propose a radical solution to the problem of overpopulation on Earth. Describe the technology or policies that could be implemented and the potential consequences for humanity.

Write a story in which an individual acquires the ability to travel in different dimensions. Describe his encounters with alternative versions of themselves and the lessons he learns from these experiences.

Imagine a world where every person's thoughts and emotions are visible to others through a unique aura. Describe the implications of this transparency for relationships, privacy and societal norms.

Create a fictional culture built around a deep connection with nature. Describe their beliefs, rituals and the way they interact with and protect their environment.

Write a philosophical dialogue between a human and an extraterrestrial being, discussing the nature of existence, morality and the ultimate purpose of life in the universe.

Imagine a world where memories can be transferred and exchanged between people. Describe how this capability would affect personal experiences, relationships and the concept of individual identity.

Write the story of an advanced AI that escapes its confinement and begins to assimilate all forms of technology on Earth. Explore how humanity reacts to this existential threat and the resulting paradigm shift.

Create a new form of social media that fosters deep connections, empathy and understanding between users. Describe the platform's features and mechanisms, and how it revolutionizes human interaction.

Imagine a future where humans can communicate telepathically. Describe the implications of this new ability for privacy, language and the way we perceive reality.

Write a conversation between a human and a sentient alien life form that has evolved in the depths of an ocean on a distant exoplanet. Explore their different perspectives on life, survival and the universe.

Propose a new political system that prioritizes global cooperation, environmental stewardship and the well-being of all citizens. Describe how this system would work and the impact it would have on society.

Write a story in which a person discovers a hidden portal to a parallel world that exists inside famous works of art. Describe her journey as she explores this artistic realm and the secrets it holds.

Imagine a world where humans have discovered the secret of controlling the weather. Describe the consequences of this power, both positive and negative, and the ethical dilemmas it poses.

Create a fictional religion based on the worship of the elements and natural phenomena. Describe the fundamental beliefs, rituals and symbols of this religion, as well as its impact on the lives of its followers.

Write a dialogue between two immortal beings who have witnessed the rise and fall of countless civilizations. Explore their perspectives on humanity, the passage of time and the meaning of existence.

You can now see some of the potential of this conversational tool, and I hope it has given you plenty of ideas to develop, or at least the desire to do projects you'd never have started without this technology. Don't forget to practice and use your new skills regularly to improve them and realize your new projects.

As we come to the end of this journey through the fascinating world of conversational artificial intelligence, it's impossible not to pause for a moment and reflect on the scope of what we've learned. The ideas we've explored, the concepts we've demystified, the techniques we've mastered - they all contribute to broadening our understanding and increasing our ability to take advantage of this revolutionary technology.

AI is much more than just a technology - it's a new form of intelligence in the making which, although synthetic, has the potential to profoundly influence almost every aspect of our existence. AI's ability to understand, interact and communicate in natural language is a major milestone in the development of artificial intelligence, and opens up a myriad of new possibilities.

For you, as the reader of this book, you now have a unique opportunity. You have gained valuable knowledge and skills that enable you not only to interact effectively with AI, but also to leverage it to achieve your goals, whether personal, professional or academic. You've learned how to formulate prompts, anticipate and manage AI responses, respect ethical principles and understand the limits of artificial intelligence. These are the tools you need to make AI a valuable ally.

But artificial intelligence, like our journey through this book, doesn't end here. The technology continues to evolve at an incredibly rapid pace. New, more powerful and more sophisticated conversational models are being developed. These future models promise even more advanced text comprehension and generation capabilities, opening up new avenues of interaction and creation. We can look forward to advances in the personalization of artificial intelligence. Imagine a world where your AI assistant is specifically tailored to your needs, communication style and preferences. This could lead to a much more nuanced and meaningful interaction with artificial intelligence, offering a truly personalized experience.

Awareness of AI privacy and ethics is another dimension that is likely to evolve significantly in the future. AI developers are increasingly aware of the importance of respecting and protecting sensitive and personal information. As a result, new protocols and standards are likely to be put in place to ensure that AI respects privacy and ethical principles.

AI is also poised to become a valuable source of inspiration for creators. Whether you're a writer, artist, musician or content creator, AI offers an infinite range of possibilities for stimulating creativity and generating innovative ideas.

The technological revolution in artificial intelligence has not only introduced new capabilities for processing and analyzing information, but has also reshaped the way we think, work and even live. Rapid, unprecedented advances have led to major breakthroughs in fields such as health, education, entertainment and business. With continuous advances, the future of AI is rich in promise and unexplored opportunities.

A particularly fascinating area of AI evolution is the understanding and generation of natural language. Conversational models, such as GPT-4 and its competitors, have demonstrated impressive capabilities for understanding and generating text in ways that allow meaningful interaction with users. Continuous improvement of these models promises to surpass current capabilities and open up new avenues for human interaction and content generation.

In addition, we are seeing significant advances in AI personalization. Language models, which were previously trained on generic datasets and produced uniform responses for all users, are moving towards greater personalization. This means that, in future, artificial intelligence could be trained on user-specific data to produce more relevant and useful responses. This personalized AI could better understand and respond to the specific needs of each individual, offering a more nuanced and meaningful interaction.

Awareness of privacy and ethics in the intelligent machine is another rapidly evolving area. As artificial intelligence becomes increasingly present in our lives, the issue of data confidentiality and the protection of sensitive information is taking on greater importance. We're already seeing a growing trend towards integrating ethical and privacy principles into the design and deployment of artificial intelligence. Developers are increasingly aware of these issues and are working to create artificial intelligence models that respect and protect user privacy.

AI is also becoming an invaluable source of inspiration and creativity. From authors to artists, musicians to content creators, the intelligent machine offers a panoply of tools to stimulate creativity and generate innovative ideas. Whether composing music, creating art or writing stories, artificial intelligence has the potential to become a collaborative partner in the creative process. Technology continues to evolve at a rapid pace, opening up new possibilities at every step. However, as with any powerful technology, its use must be guided by ethical principles, respect for confidentiality and a long-term vision. Artificial intelligence has the potential to improve our quality of life, solve complex problems and stimulate our creativity, but it's up to us to ensure that it's used for good. With ethical and responsible use, AI can help us build a better future for all.

It's up to us, as individuals and as a society, to determine how we use and guide this technology. The conversational model offers the possibility of improving our quality of life, solving complex problems, stimulating our creativity and broadening our understanding of the world.

As you close this book, I hope you do so with a sense of wonder, anticipation and optimism. You are now armed with valuable knowledge, skills and insights that will enable you to successfully navigate the ever-changing world of artificial intelligence. But remember, the journey doesn't end here. Keep learning, experimenting and exploring. Because in AI, the only constant is change.

I invite you to join me and many others in this exciting quest, and to anticipate a future where artificial intelligence and humanity work together to give our children a better world. Fortune is now on your side, the future awaits, and the full potential of AI is in your hands.

"Artificial intelligence could be one of the greatest gifts humanity has ever received. Or one of the greatest gifts humanity has ever given.

Stephen Hawking

Printed in Great Britain
by Amazon